TUNISIAN
CROCHET STITCH
Dictionary

TUNISIAN CROCHET STITCH
Dictionary

150 essential stitches with actual-size swatches, charts, and step-by-step photos

Anna Nikipirowicz

Landauer Publishing

A QUARTO BOOK

ISBN 978-1-6398-1026-0

Copyright © 2023 Quarto Publishing plc, an imprint of The Quarto Group

This edition published in 2023 by Landauer, *www.landauerpub.com*, an imprint of Fox Chapel Publishing, 800-457-9112, 903 Square Street, Mount Joy, PA 17552.

We are always looking for talented authors. To submit an idea, please send a brief inquiry to acquisitions@ foxchapelpublishing.com.

Conceived, edited, and designed by Quarto Publishing plc an imprint of The Quarto Group The Old Brewery 6 Blundell Street London N7 9BH www.quartoknows.com

QUAR: 355400

Editor & designer: Michelle Pickering
Technical editor: Linda Brown
Photographers: Nicki Dowey (beauty shots & cover), Anna Nikipirowicz (step-by-steps), Phil Wilkins (swatches)
Illustrators: Kuo Kang Chen (techniques), Anna Nikipirowicz (charts)
Color correction: Clippingpatharts
Art director: Martina Calvio
Managing editor: Lesley Henderson

Printed in China
First printing

MIX
Paper from responsible sources
FSC® C016973

contents

Directory of Stitches   **14**

Basic Stitches

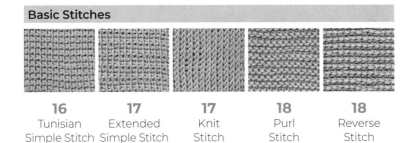

This illustrated contents list shows photographs of all 150 stitches in the directory. Use it help you choose which patterns to make. Turn to the page number in bold below each photograph for full instructions.

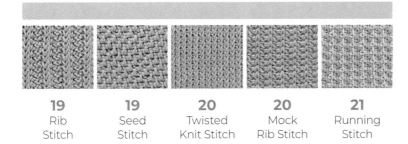

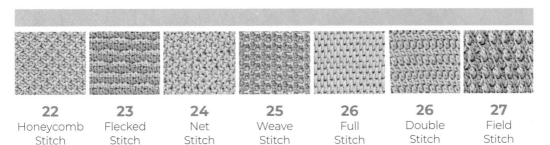

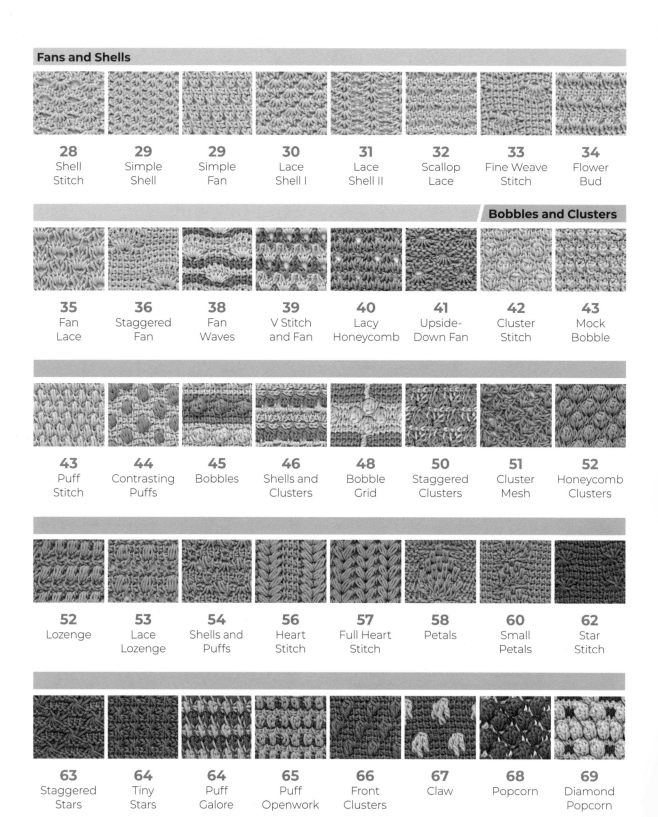

Fans and Shells

28 Shell Stitch

29 Simple Shell

29 Simple Fan

30 Lace Shell I

31 Lace Shell II

32 Scallop Lace

33 Fine Weave Stitch

34 Flower Bud

Bobbles and Clusters

35 Fan Lace

36 Staggered Fan

38 Fan Waves

39 V Stitch and Fan

40 Lacy Honeycomb

41 Upside-Down Fan

42 Cluster Stitch

43 Mock Bobble

43 Puff Stitch

44 Contrasting Puffs

45 Bobbles

46 Shells and Clusters

48 Bobble Grid

50 Staggered Clusters

51 Cluster Mesh

52 Honeycomb Clusters

52 Lozenge

53 Lace Lozenge

54 Shells and Puffs

56 Heart Stitch

57 Full Heart Stitch

58 Petals

60 Small Petals

62 Star Stitch

63 Staggered Stars

64 Tiny Stars

64 Puff Galore

65 Puff Openwork

66 Front Clusters

67 Claw

68 Popcorn

69 Diamond Popcorn

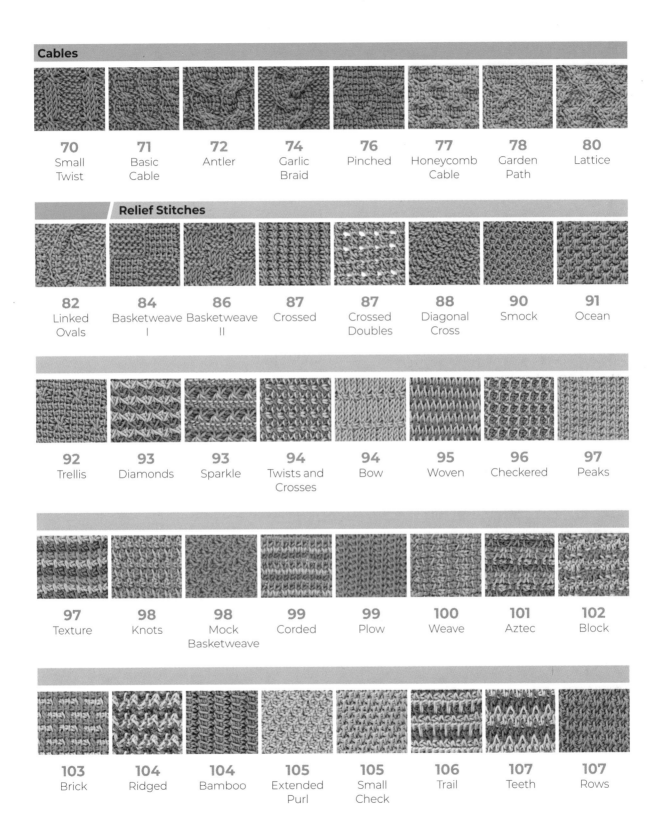

Cables

70 Small Twist

71 Basic Cable

72 Antler

74 Garlic Braid

76 Pinched

77 Honeycomb Cable

78 Garden Path

80 Lattice

Relief Stitches

82 Linked Ovals

84 Basketweave I

86 Basketweave II

87 Crossed

87 Crossed Doubles

88 Diagonal Cross

90 Smock

91 Ocean

92 Trellis

93 Diamonds

93 Sparkle

94 Twists and Crosses

94 Bow

95 Woven

96 Checkered

97 Peaks

97 Texture

98 Knots

98 Mock Basketweave

99 Corded

99 Plow

100 Weave

101 Aztec

102 Block

103 Brick

104 Ridged

104 Bamboo

105 Extended Purl

105 Small Check

106 Trail

107 Teeth

107 Rows

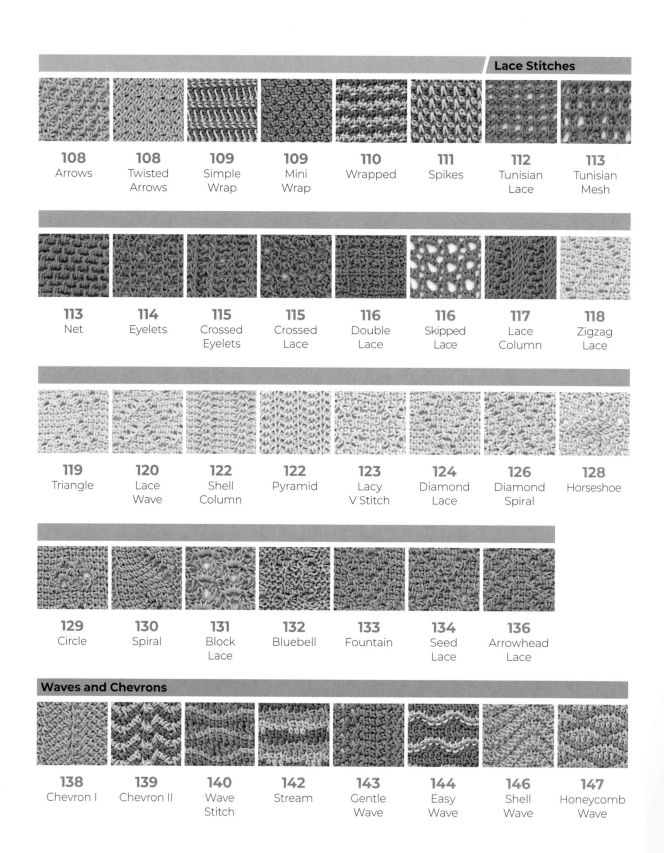

108 Arrows

108 Twisted Arrows

109 Simple Wrap

109 Mini Wrap

110 Wrapped

111 Spikes

112 Tunisian Lace

113 Tunisian Mesh

113 Net

114 Eyelets

115 Crossed Eyelets

115 Crossed Lace

116 Double Lace

116 Skipped Lace

117 Lace Column

118 Zigzag Lace

119 Triangle

120 Lace Wave

122 Shell Column

122 Pyramid

123 Lacy V Stitch

124 Diamond Lace

126 Diamond Spiral

128 Horseshoe

129 Circle

130 Spiral

131 Block Lace

132 Bluebell

133 Fountain

134 Seed Lace

136 Arrowhead Lace

Waves and Chevrons

138 Chevron I

139 Chevron II

140 Wave Stitch

142 Stream

143 Gentle Wave

144 Easy Wave

146 Shell Wave

147 Honeycomb Wave

Embellishments

148 Cross Stitch	149 Duplicate Stitch	149 Surface Slip Stitch	150 Surface Slip Stitch over Mesh	151 Weaving	151 Beaded Stitch

Edgings

152 V Stitch Edging	152 Wave Edging	153 Fan Edging	153 Picot Edging	154 Striped Edging	154 Puff Edging	155 Lace Edging	155 Seed Edging

Introduction

Crochet and knitting have always been my first passion, and I have to admit that very often crochet won in my favors. I have been exploring, designing, and constantly learning new techniques for quite a few years now. I owe my love for both of these crafts to my wonderful late Mum, Lucy.

A few years ago I tried Tunisian (or Afghan) crochet for the first time. It was a pattern for a scarf I found in a vintage magazine, and I was wowed. It is a cross between regular crochet and knitting that is totally addictive. It resembles crochet because you work with a hook, but a hook that is longer than the one you would use for standard crochet, and it starts with chains. It also resembles knitting, because you gather all the stitches onto the hook; you do that on forward passes, then work those stitches off the hook on return passes. Unlike in knitting or standard crochet, in Tunisian crochet you only work on the right side of the work, which a lot of people find incredibly useful. The fabric produced with Tunisian crochet is closer to that of a knitted fabric in look, but in feel it is closer to crochet as it is thicker.

Tunisian crochet has been around for a very long time. It is known that Queen Victoria of England favored the craft, and it was even called "Royal Princess Knitting" in her honor. Sadly, by the 1930s Tunisian crochet had lost its popularity. There were still patterns and books published on this craft, but nowhere near as many as on knitting and crochet. In recent times, however, it has seen a huge revival and I could not be happier. This superb craft deserves a place at the top among the favorites.

I have included a wide variety of stitches in this book, from basic to more complicated, so that there is something for everyone to try. I have used my crochet knowledge to experiment with creating stitches such as popcorns and bobbles, and my knitting knowledge to create the cables and lace.

It is a huge honor to bring to you this wonderful dictionary with 150 of my favorite Tunisian crochet stitches. Each stitch is accompanied by a finished example, written instructions, charts, and step-by-step photographs. I hope that they will inspire your creativity and that you will enjoy trying something new, like adding a new stitch to your work or combining them to create beautiful projects.

Anna x

About This Book

The main chapter of this book is the Directory of Stitches (pages 14–155), featuring step-by-step instructions for 150 Tunisian crochet stitches ranging from shells, clusters, and cables to lace, chevrons, and edgings. If you are new to Tunisian crochet or need to brush up your crochet skills at any point, at the back of the book you will find the Tunisian Crochet Skills chapter (pages 156–173). There you will find information on Tunisian crochet basics, from choosing yarn and holding the hook to working stitches and variations.

KEY FACTS

Foundation chain and multiple: Tunisian crochet always starts with a foundation chain. Use the multiple provided at the beginning of the pattern to calculate how many chains to make in your foundation chain (see page 163).

Basic stitches: All of the stitch patterns use Tunisian simple stitch, so practice this first (page 16). Other key basic stitches are Tunisian knit, purl, full, double, and slip stitch. These are explained in the basic stitches section at the beginning of the directory (pages 16–27); if you need a reminder thereafter, see page 165.

Special stitches: Advanced or special stitches are explained with clear written instructions near the beginning of each pattern. These are also used to help make some patterns shorter or easier to follow and memorize.

Step and chart numbers: The step numbers in the patterns correspond to the numbers on the charts. Each row of Tunisian crochet consists of a forward pass and a return pass (see page 164). All odd numbers are forward passes; all even numbers are return passes.

Final step: The final step of each pattern indicates which steps to repeat to continue the pattern.

Charts indicate the section that forms the repeat of the pattern, and always include at least one full pattern repeat.

Guidelines for the length of foundation chain required are listed. See page 163 for more on this.

Special stitch instructions are provided near the beginning of each pattern when they are needed.

Written step-by-step instructions guide you through the creation of the stitch. Make sure that you begin with the correct number of foundation chains and follow the instructions exactly. The terminology of crochet can be confusing at first. A list of abbreviations is given on page 170 at the back of the book.

READING THE PATTERNS AND CHARTS

The 150 Tunisian crochet stitches that make up the stitch directory, with written instructions and charts, will help you master a wide range of Tunisian crochet skills. Organized into nine families of stitches and clearly numbered, you can dip in and out of the directory or work your way through a particular section to develop your skills in that area.

Stitches are divided into stitch families and clearly numbered.

Swatches shown at approximately actual size provide a great visual for how the finished stitch will look.

Symbol charts in the color of the swatch provide a visual map for working the stitch. Symbols indicate the different stitches and how they are placed in relation to each other. A list of symbols can be found on pages 170–173. Charts represent the right side of the work. Forward passes are numbered at the right and read from right to left. Return passes are numbered at the left and read from left to right.

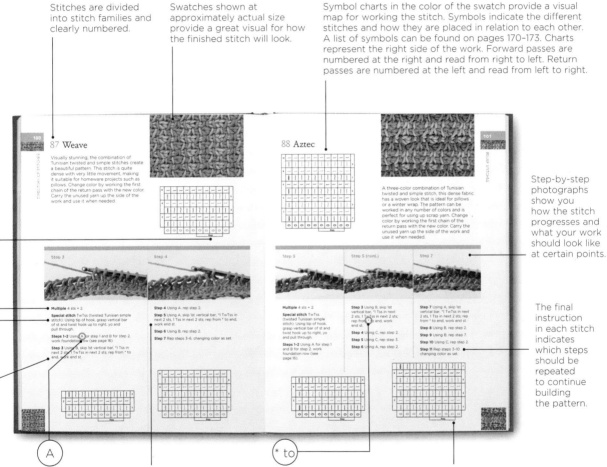

Step-by-step photographs show you how the stitch progresses and what your work should look like at certain points.

The final instruction in each stitch indicates which steps should be repeated to continue building the pattern.

A Different colored yarns are allocated a letter in patterns that use more than one color.

At the beginning of each forward pass, the loop on the hook counts as the first stitch, so don't work into the stitch immediately below it (unless you want to increase). The end stitch is always worked the same and is treated separately in the patterns. See page 164 for more information on the first and last stitches.

* to Asterisks * within the instructions indicate a point from which instructions are repeated. For example, "rep from * to end" means you should repeat the instructions after the * across the whole pass as far as the end stitch. Where instructions given after the * do not fit exactly, the instruction will reflect this. For example, "*1 Tss in next st, 1 Tks in next 3 sts; rep from * to end, ending last rep with 1 Tks in next 2 sts" means repeat the instructions after the * but on the last repeat work 1 Tks in next 2 sts instead of next 3 sts.

The charts for some stitches are broken down to help you locate the specific part of the chart that relates to the instructions in that step or steps. Previous steps are shown in gray so you can see how the chart and the stitch build up.

1 Directory of Stitches

Dive into the directory of 150 Tunisian crochet stitches and learn how to build a sturdy and hard-wearing fabric from basic Tunisian stitches, create a multicolored pattern of waves and chevrons, make a beautiful and delicate lace fabric, or embellish your pieces with clusters, bobbles, or cables. The directory is divided into nine families of stitches to help you to easily find the perfect one to suit your project. Whether you dip in and out or work your way through a complete section to really master one technique, get ready to make some stunning Tunisian crochet creations.

1 Tunisian Simple Stitch

This stitch is the basis for all Tunisian crochet patterns. It creates a beautiful fabric with fair drape, and is perfect for accessories, garments, and homewares. It has a tendency to curl; using a hook larger than recommended for the yarn will help.

KEY FACTS

Foundation row: All Tunisian stitch patterns start with the same foundation row as Tunisian simple stitch (steps 1–2), unless specified otherwise.

Working the end stitch: After the foundation row, work the end stitch of each row by inserting the hook under both the front and back vertical bars of the stitch at the edge of the fabric. The patterns treat the end stitch separately; work 1 Tss in the end stitch unless specified otherwise.

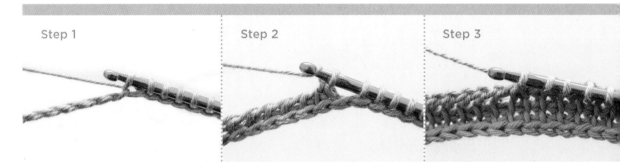

Step 1	Step 2	Step 3

Multiple Any number of sts.

Special stitch Tss (Tunisian simple stitch): Insert hook from right to left under front vertical bar of st (or into bump at back of ch when working into foundation ch), yo and pull through.

Step 1 (forward pass) 1 Tss in 2nd ch from hook and in each ch to end.

Step 2 (return pass) Yo and pull through 1 loop on hook, *yo and pull through 2 loops; rep from * until 1 loop left on hook.

Note Steps 1 and 2 are your foundational row. You will come back to this when doing other stitches. In addition, step 2 is the standard return pass for all rows of Tunisian crochet unless a different instruction is provided in the pattern.

Step 3 Loop on hook counts as 1st st, so skip 1st vertical bar, 1 Tss in each st to end, work end st.

Step 4 Rep step 2.

Step 5 Rep steps 3–4.

Note The final step of each pattern indicates which steps to repeat to continue building the pattern.

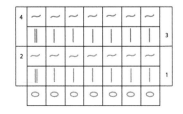

2 Extended Simple Stitch

A variation of Tunisian simple stitch with the addition of a chain, this pattern creates a beautiful fabric with fair drape and an airy feel. It is perfect for accessories and garments.

3 Knit Stitch

This looks like knitted stockinette, but creates a more dense and sturdy fabric. It curls a lot and requires blocking; using a hook larger than recommended for the yarn will help. It is a great stitch to use for garments, accessories, and in combination with other Tunisian stitches.

Step 1

Step 3

Multiple Any number of sts.

Special stitch ETss (extended Tunisian simple stitch): Insert hook from right to left under front vertical bar of st, yo and pull through, ch 1.

Steps 1–2 Work foundation row (see page 16).

Step 3 Ch 1, skip 1st vertical bar, 1 ETss in each st to end, work end st.

Step 4 Rep step 2.

Step 5 Rep steps 3–4.

Step 2

Step 3

Multiple Any number of sts.

Special stitch Tks (Tunisian knit stitch): Insert hook from front to back through center of st between vertical bars, yo and pull through.

Steps 1–2 Work foundation row (see page 16).

Step 3 Skip 1st vertical bar, 1 Tks in each st to end, work end st.

Step 4 Rep step 2.

Step 5 Rep steps 3–4.

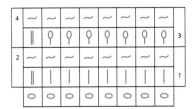

4 Purl Stitch

This stitch closely resembles purl stitch in knitting. It produces fabric with good drape and full of texture, perfect for accessories such as scarves and shawls. The fabric is also hard-wearing, making it ideal for homewares like blankets and pillows.

5 Reverse Stitch

This stitch looks similar to Tunisian purl stitch. Likewise, the hard-wearing fabric is full of texture, has good drape, and is suitable for accessories and homewares.

Step 1

Step 3

Step 2

Step 3

Multiple Any number of sts.

Special stitch Tps (Tunisian purl stitch): Bring yarn to front, insert hook from right to left under front vertical bar of st, take yarn across front of st to back of work, yo and pull through.

Steps 1–2 Work foundation row (see page 16).

Step 3 Skip 1st vertical bar, 1 Tps in each st to end, work end st.

Step 4 Rep step 2.

Step 5 Rep steps 3–4.

Multiple Any number of sts.

Special stitch Trs (Tunisian reverse stitch): With yarn and hook at back, insert hook from right to left under back vertical bar of st, yo and pull through.

Steps 1–2 Work foundation row (see page 16).

Step 3 Skip 1st vertical bar, 1 Trs in each st to end, work end st.

Step 4 Rep step 2.

Step 5 Rep steps 3–4.

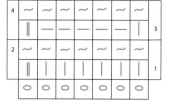

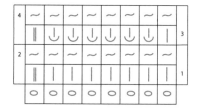

6 Rib Stitch

Alternating columns of Tunisian knit and purl stitches create a fabric that looks like knitted rib, and is likewise perfect for cuffs on garments and edgings. Try different combinations of this stitch, such as 1 x 1 or 3 x 3 rib.

7 Seed Stitch

This pattern of alternating Tunisian knit and purl stitches creates an interesting fabric that is perfect for garments, accessories, and homewares. It is identical to seed stitch in knitting.

Step 3	Step 3 (cont.)

Multiple 4 sts + 2.

Special stitches
Tks (Tunisian knit stitch): Insert hook from front to back through center of st between vertical bars, yo and pull through.

Tps (Tunisian purl stitch): Bring yarn to front, insert hook from right to left under front vertical bar of st, take yarn across front of st to back of work, yo and pull through.

Steps 1–2 Work foundation row (see page 16).

Step 3 Skip 1st vertical bar, *1 Tps in next 2 sts, 1 Tks in next 2 sts; rep from * to end, work end st.

Step 4 Rep step 2.

Step 5 Rep steps 3–4.

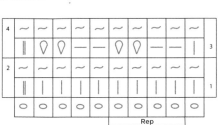

Step 3	Step 5

Multiple 2 sts + 2.

Special stitches
As left.

Steps 1–2 Work foundation row (see page 16).

Step 3 Skip 1st vertical bar, *1 Tks in next st, 1 Tps in next st; rep from * to end, work end st.

Step 4 Rep step 2.

Step 5 Skip 1st vertical bar, *1 Tps in next st, 1 Tks in next st; rep from * to end, work end st.

Step 6 Rep step 2.

Step 7 Rep steps 3–6.

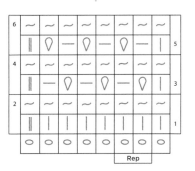

8 Twisted Knit Stitch

This dense stitch creates a fabric with very little drape. It has a lovely texture and works well for sturdy homewares, such as baskets and pillows. It curls a lot and requires blocking. Using a larger hook will provide more drape to the fabric.

9 Mock Rib Stitch

This stitch gives the illusion of 1 x 1 rib. It is a combination of Tunisian simple stitch and twisted simple stitch. It creates fabric that is quite dense, but has good drape.

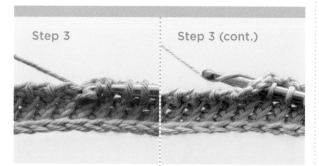

Step 3

Step 3 (cont.)

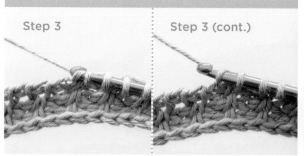

Step 3

Step 3 (cont.)

Multiple Any number of sts.

Special stitch TwTks (twisted Tunisian knit stitch): Using tip of hook, pull front vertical bar of st to right to reveal back vertical bar, insert hook from front to back through center of st between vertical bars, yo and pull through.

Steps 1–2 Work foundation row (see page 16).

Step 3 Skip 1st vertical bar, 1 TwTks in each st to end, work end st.

Step 4 Rep step 2.

Step 5 Rep steps 3–4.

Multiple 2 sts + 2.

Special stitch TwTss (twisted Tunisian simple stitch): Using tip of hook, grasp vertical bar of st and twist hook up to right, yo and pull through.

Steps 1–2 Work foundation row (see page 16).

Step 3 Skip 1st vertical bar, *1 TwTss in next st, 1 Tss in next st; rep from to end, work end st.

Step 4 Rep step 2.

Step 5 Rep steps 3–4.

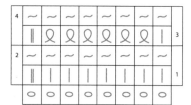

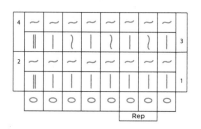

10 Running Stitch

A combination of Tunisian simple and slip stitches, this pattern creates a dense fabric with little drape, so using a hook at least two sizes larger is recommended. The stitch looks beautiful in single or multiple colors, and is perfect for homewares. Change color on the return pass when two loops are left on the hook; finish off the pass with the new color. Carry the unused yarn up the side of the work and use it when needed.

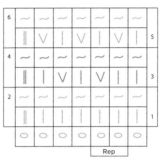

Step 3

Step 4

Step 5

Multiple 2 sts + 3.

Special stitch Tslst (Tunisian slip stitch): Insert hook from right to left under front vertical bar of st, leave bar on hook without working it.

Steps 1–2 Using A, work foundation row (see page 16).

Step 3 Using B, skip 1st vertical bar, *1 Tss in next st, 1 Tslst in next st; rep from * to last st, 1 Tss in next st, work end st.

Step 4 Using B, rep step 2.

Step 5 Using A, skip 1st vertical bar, *1 Tslst in next st, 1 Tss in next st; rep from * to last st, 1 Tslst in next st, work end st.

Step 6 Using A, rep step 2.

Step 7 Rep steps 3–6, changing color as set.

11 Honeycomb Stitch

This beautiful stitch produces a fabric full of interesting texture. It is created by alternating Tunisian purl and simple stitches. The fabric has good drape and is perfect for garments and accessories.

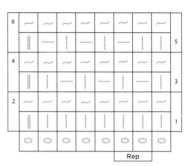

Step 2

Multiple 2 sts + 2.

Special stitch Tps (Tunisian purl stitch): Bring yarn to front, insert hook from right to left under front vertical bar of st, take yarn across front of st to back of work, yo and pull through.

Steps 1–2 Work foundation row (see page 16).

Step 3

Step 3 Skip 1st vertical bar, *1 Tps in next st, 1 Tss in next st; rep from * to end, work end st.

Step 4 Rep step 2.

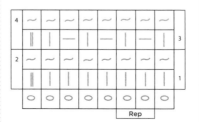

Step 5

Step 5 Skip 1st vertical bar, *1 Tss in next st, 1 Tps in next st; rep from * to end, work end st.

Step 6 Rep step 2.

Step 7 Rep steps 3–6.

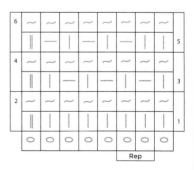

12 Flecked Stitch

This pattern creates a dense fabric with little drape. It is produced using Tunisian simple and slip stitches to create the fleck effect. Because of the tightness of the stitch, it is perfect for homewares such as pillows and wall hangings. To give the fabric more movement, use a hook two sizes larger than recommended for the yarn. Change color on the return pass when two loops are left on the hook; finish off the pass with the new color. Carry the unused yarn up the side of the work and use it when needed.

Step 2

Multiple 4 sts + 4.

Special stitch Tslst (Tunisian slip stitch): Insert hook from right to left under front vertical bar of st, leave bar on hook without working it.

Steps 1–2 Using A, work foundation row (see page 16).

Step 3

Step 3 Using B, skip 1st vertical bar, *1 Tslst in next st, 1 Tss in next 3 sts; rep from * to last 2 sts, 1 Tslst in next st, 1 Tss in next st, work end st.

Step 4 Using B, rep step 2.

Step 5

Step 5 Using A, skip 1st vertical bar, 1 Tss in next 2 sts, *1 Tslst in next st, 1 Tss in next 3 sts; rep from * to end, work end st.

Step 6 Using A, rep step 2.

Step 7 Rep steps 3–6, changing color as set.

13 Net Stitch

Although similar to Tunisian seed stitch, this pattern produces a fabric with more drape. It is perfect for making garments and accessories. The pattern is constructed from a combination of Tunisian knit stitch and knit stitch purled.

Step 3

Step 5

Multiple 2 sts + 2.

Special stitches Tks (Tunisian knit stitch): Insert hook from front to back through center of st between vertical bars, yo and pull through.

Tks purled (Tunisian knit stitch purled): Bring yarn to front, insert hook as for Tks, take yarn across front of st to back of work, yo and pull through.

Steps 1–2 Work foundation row (see page 16).

Step 3 Skip 1st vertical bar, *1 Tks in next st, 1 Tks purled in next st; rep from * to end, work end st.

Step 4 Rep step 2.

Step 5 Skip 1st vertical bar, *1 Tks purled in next st, 1 Tks in next st; rep from * to end, work end st.

Step 6 Rep step 2.

Step 7 Rep steps 3–6.

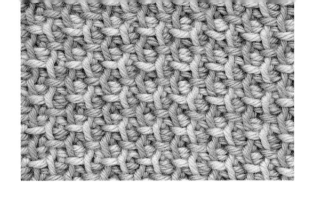

14 Weave Stitch

A wonderful combination of Tunisian simple and purled slip stitches, this pattern creates fabric with fair drape. The stitch looks beautiful in single or multiple colors, and is perfect for homewares, garments, and accessories. Change color on the return pass when two loops are left on the hook; finish off the pass with the new color. Carry the unused yarn up the side of the work and use it when needed.

Step 3

Step 5

Multiple 2 sts + 2.

Special stitch Tslst purled (Tunisian slip stitch purled): Bring yarn to front, insert hook from right to left under front vertical bar of st, leave bar on hook without working it, take yarn across front of st to back of work.

Steps 1–2 Using A, work foundation row (see page 16).

Step 3 Using B, skip 1st vertical bar, *1 Tslst purled in next st, 1 Tss in next st; rep from * to end, work end st.

Step 4 Using B, rep step 2.

Step 5 Using A, skip 1st vertical bar, *1 Tss in next st, 1 Tslst purled in next st; rep from * to end, work end st.

Step 6 Using A, rep step 2.

Step 7 Rep steps 3–6, changing color as set.

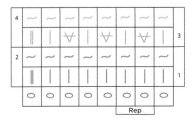

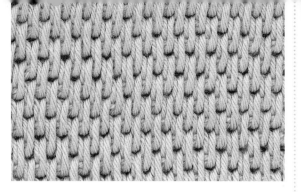

15 Full Stitch

Also known as mesh or goblin stitch, this gorgeous fabric has good drape, but it curls a lot and requires good blocking. It is worked in the spaces between the vertical bars. Check the number of stitches after each forward pass to help you keep the pattern correct and the edges straight.

16 Double Stitch

This lovely, loose stitch produces a drapey and airy fabric that is perfect for accessories such as shawls and scarves. It is created by wrapping the yarn over the hook before inserting the hook under the first vertical bar.

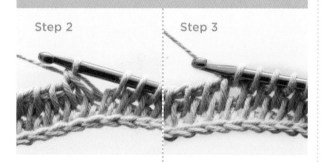

Step 2

Step 3

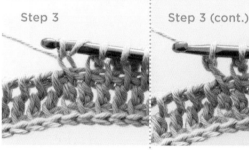

Step 3

Step 3 (cont.)

Multiple Any number of sts.

Special stitch
Tfs (Tunisian full stitch): Insert hook from front to back in sp between sts, yo and pull through.

Steps 1–2 Work foundation row (see page 16).

Step 3 Skip 1st vertical bar, 1 Tfs in sp between 1st and 2nd sts, 1 Tfs in each sp to last sp, skip last sp, work end st.

Step 4 Rep step 2.

Step 5 Skip 1st vertical bar and sp, 1 Tfs in sp between 2nd and 3rd sts, 1 Tfs in each sp to end, work end st.

Step 6 Rep step 2.

Step 7 Rep steps 3–6.

Multiple Any number of sts.

Special stitch
Tdc (Tunisian double crochet): Yo, insert hook from right to left under front vertical bar of st, yo and pull through, yo and pull through 2 loops on hook.

Steps 1–2 Work foundation row (see page 16).

Step 3 Ch 1, skip 1st vertical bar, 1 Tdc in each st to end, 1 Tdc in end st.

Step 4 Rep step 2.

Step 5 Rep steps 3–4.

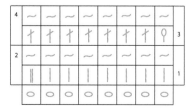

17 Field Stitch

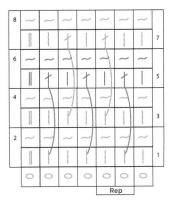

Beautifully textured, this stitch produces a fabric with wonderful drape that is perfect for making garments and accessories. Change color on the return pass when two loops are left on the hook; finish off the pass with the new color. Carry the unused yarn up the side of the work and use it when needed.

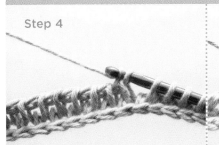

Step 4

Step 5

Step 7

Multiple 2 sts + 1.

Special stitch Long Tdc (long Tunisian double crochet): Yo, insert hook from right to left under front vertical bar of next st 2 rows below, yo and pull through, yo and pull through 2 loops on hook.

Steps 1–2 Using A, work foundation row (see page 16).

Step 3 Using A, skip 1st vertical bar, 1 Tss in each st to end, work end st.

Step 4 Using A, rep step 2.

Step 5 Using B, skip 1st vertical bar, 1 Long Tdc, *1 Tss in next st, 1 Long Tdc; rep from * to end, work end st.

Step 6 Using B, rep step 2.

Step 7 Using A, skip 1st vertical bar, 1 Tss in next st, *1 Long Tdc, 1 Tss in next st; rep from * to end, work end st.

Step 8 Using A, rep step 2.

Step 9 Rep steps 5–8, changing color as set.

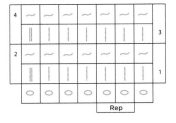

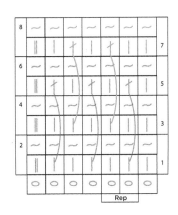

18 Shell Stitch

This lovely shell stitch with beautiful drape is perfect for lacy garments and accessories. The shells are worked on the return pass. When counting stitches off the hook when creating shells, the loop on the hook counts as 1.

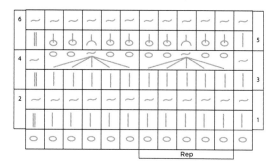

Step 3

Step 4

Step 5

Multiple 5 sts + 2.

Steps 1–2 Work foundation row (see page 16).

Step 3 Skip 1st vertical bar, 1 Tss in each st to end, work end st.

Step 4 Yo and pull through 1 loop on hook, *ch 2, yo and pull through 6 loops (shell made), ch 2; rep from * until 2 loops left on hook, yo and pull through 2 loops.

Step 5 Skip 1st vertical bar, 1 Tss in each ch and top of shell to end, work end st.

Step 6 Rep step 2.

Step 7 Rep steps 3–6.

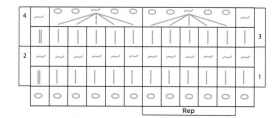

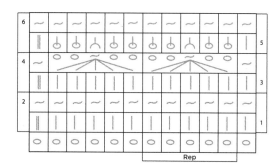

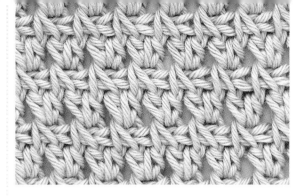

19 Simple Shell

Small shells create a fabric with good drape and a lacy feel. The shells are worked on the return pass. When counting stitches off the hook when creating shells, the loop on the hook counts as 1.

20 Simple Fan

This simple stitch creates a lacy and open fabric with plenty of drape. The pattern is created by working two Tunisian double crochets into two Tunisian simple stitches at the same time.

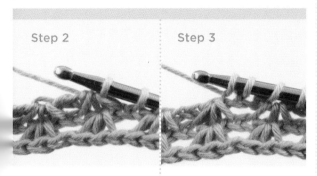

Step 2

Step 3

Multiple 3 sts + 2.

Step 1 1 Tss in 2nd ch from hook and in each ch to end.

Step 2 Yo and pull through 1 loop on hook, *ch 1, yo and pull through 4 loops (shell made), ch 1; rep from * until 2 loops left on hook, yo and pull through 2 loops.

Step 3 Skip 1st vertical bar, 1 Tss in each ch and top of shell to end, work end st.

Step 4 Rep steps 2–3, ending with step 2.

Step 3

Step 3 (cont.)

Multiple 2 sts + 3.

Steps 1–2 Work foundation row (see page 16).

Step 3 Ch 1, skip 1st vertical bar, *2 Tdc in next 2 sts at same time (insert hook under front vertical bar of both sts for each Tdc); rep from * to last st, 1 Tdc in next st, 1 Tdc in end st.

Step 4 Rep step 2.

Step 5 Ch 1, skip 1st vertical bar, 1 Tdc in next st, *2 Tdc in next 2 sts at same time; rep from * to end, 1 Tdc in end st.

Step 6 Rep steps 2–5, ending with step 2.

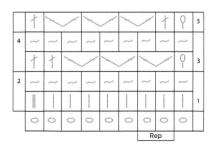

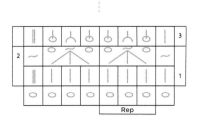

21 Lace Shell I

An elegant stitch with lots of drape, this pattern looks lovely in lacy yarns. The shells are placed in between lower shells on every return pass. When counting stitches off the hook when creating shells, the loop on the hook counts as 1.

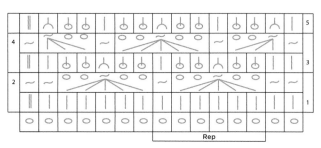

Step 2

Step 3

Step 4

Multiple 6 sts + 3.

Step 1 1 Tss in 2nd ch from hook and in each ch to end.

Step 2 Yo and pull through 1 loop on hook, *yo and pull through 2 loops, ch 2, yo and pull through 6 loops (shell made), ch 2; rep from * until 3 loops left on hook, [yo and pull through 2 loops] twice.

Step 3 Skip 1st vertical bar, *1 Tss in each st, ch, and top of shell to end, work end st.

Step 4 Yo and pull through 1 loop on hook, yo and pull through 4 loops (shell made), ch 2, *yo and pull through 2 loops, ch 2, yo and pull through 6 loops

(shell made), ch 2; rep from * until 6 loops left on hook, yo and pull through 2 loops, ch 2, yo and pull through 4 loops (shell made), yo and pull through 2 loops.

Step 5 Rep step 3.

Step 6 Rep steps 2–5, ending with step 2.

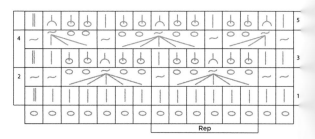

22 Lace Shell II

Producing an airy fabric with very good drape, this stitch is perfect for summer accessories. The shells are worked on the return pass. When counting stitches off the hook when creating shells, the loop on the hook counts as 1.

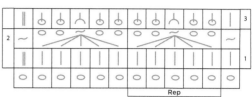

Step 1

Multiple 5 sts + 2.

Step 1 1 Tss in 2nd ch from hook and in each ch to end.

Step 2

Step 2 Yo and pull through 1 loop on hook, *ch 2, yo and pull through 6 loops (shell made), ch 2; rep from * until 2 loops left on hook, yo and pull through 2 loops.

Step 3

Step 3 Skip 1st vertical bar, *1 Tss in each ch and top of shell to end, work end st.

Step 4 Rep steps 2–3, ending with step 2.

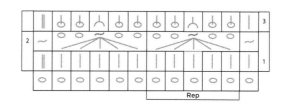

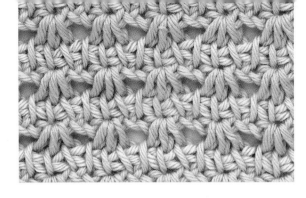

23 Scallop Lace

This pretty stitch looks wonderful worked in two colors or just one. The fabric has good drape and a light feel, perfect for lacy garments and accessories. When counting stitches off the hook when creating shells, the loop on the hook counts as 1. Change color on the return pass when two loops are left on the hook; finish off the pass with the new color.

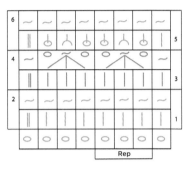

Step 4

Step 5

Step 6

Multiple 3 sts + 2.

Steps 1–2 Using A, work foundation row (see page 16).

Step 3 Using B, skip 1st vertical bar, *1 Tss in each st to end, work end st.

Step 4 Using B, yo and pull through 1 loop on hook, *ch 1, yo and pull through 4 loops (shell made), ch 1;

rep from * until 2 loops left on hook, yo and pull through 2 loops.

Step 5 Using A, skip 1st vertical bar, *1 Tss in each ch and top of shell to end, work end st.

Step 6 Using A, rep step 2.

Step 7 Rep steps 3–6, changing color as set.

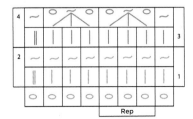

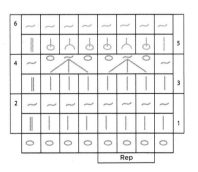

24 Fine Weave Stitch

This easy-to-memorize pattern produces a fabric with fair drape that is perfect for home and winter accessories. Rows of Tunisian simple stitch are interrupted with fans of Tunisian double crochet.

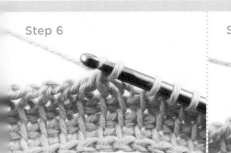

Step 6

Step 7

Step 8

Multiple 10 sts + 2.

Special stitch Fan: Inserting hook as for Tks, work 5 Tdc in same st.

Steps 1–2 Work foundation row (see page 16).

Step 3 Skip 1st vertical bar, *1 Tss in each st to end, work end st.

Steps 4, 6, 8, 10, 12 Rep step 2.

Step 5 Rep step 3.

Step 7 Skip 1st vertical bar, *skip next 2 sts, Fan in next st, skip next 2 sts, 1 Tss in next 5 sts; rep from * to end, work end st.

Steps 9, 11 Rep step 3.

Step 13 Skip 1st vertical bar, *1 Tss in next 5 sts, skip next 2 sts, Fan in next st, skip next 2 sts; rep from * to

end, work end st.

Step 14 Rep steps 2–13, ending with step 2.

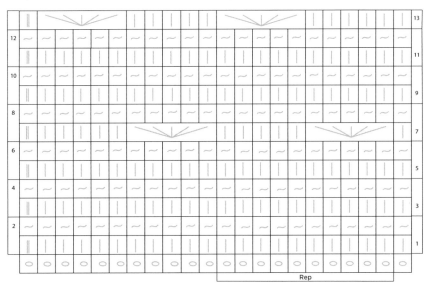

25 Flower Bud

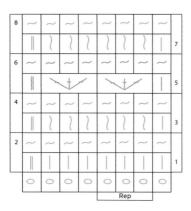

This delicate stitch created by small fans produces an airy fabric with fair drape that is perfect for summer garments and accessories. The rows of fans are worked into rows of twisted Tunisian simple stitch. Change color on the return pass when two loops are left on the hook; finish off the pass with the new color.

Step 3

Step 3 (cont.)

Step 5

Multiple 3 sts + 2.

Special stitches TwTss (twisted Tunisian simple stitch): Using tip of hook, grasp vertical bar of st and twist hook up to right, yo and pull through.

Fan: Inserting hook as for Tks, work 3 Tdc in same st.

Steps 1–2 Using A, work foundation row (see page 16).

Step 3 Using A, skip 1st vertical bar, 1 TwTss in each st to end, work end st.

Step 4 Using A, rep step 2.

Step 5 Using B, skip 1st vertical bar, *skip next st, Fan in next st, skip next

st; rep from * to end, work end st.

Step 6 Using B, rep step 2.

Steps 7–8 Using A, rep steps 3–4.

Step 9 Rep steps 5–8, changing color as set.

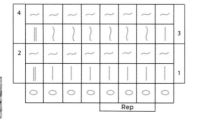

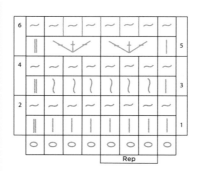

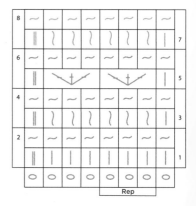

26 Fan Lace

This simple fan pattern looks striking in one or two colors. It is a very pretty stitch and works well for items that require reversible fabric. It is fairly airy with good drape. The fans of Tunisian double crochet are worked on the forward pass.

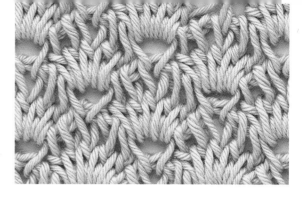

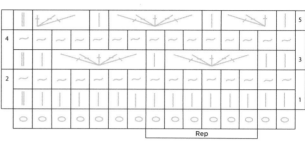

Step 3

Step 4

Step 5

Multiple 6 sts + 3.

Special stitches Fan: Inserting hook as for Tks, work 5 Tdc in same st.

Half Fan: Inserting hook as for Tks, work 3 Tdc in same st.

Steps 1–2 Work foundation row (see page 16).

Step 3 Skip 1st vertical bar, 1 Tss in next st, *skip next 2 sts, Fan in next st, skip next 2 sts, 1 Tss in next st; rep from * to end, work end st.

Step 4 Rep step 2.

Step 5 Skip 1st vertical bar, Half Fan in next st, skip next 2 sts, 1 Tss in next st, *skip next 2 sts, Fan in next st, skip next 2 sts, 1 Tss in next st; rep from * to last 3 sts, skip next 2 sts, Half Fan in next st, work end st.

Step 6 Rep steps 2–5, ending with step 2.

27 Staggered Fan

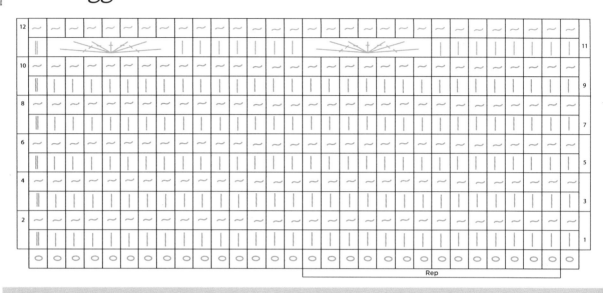

Step 11

Step 12

Step 21

Multiple 14 sts + 2.

Special stitch Fan: Inserting hook as for Tks, work 7 Tdc in same st.

Steps 1–2 Using A, work foundation row (see page 16).

Step 3 Using A, skip 1st vertical bar, 1 Tss in each st to end, work end st.

Step 4 Using A, rep step 2.

Steps 5–10 Using A, rep steps 3–4.

Step 11 Using B, skip 1st vertical bar, *1 Tss in next 7 sts, skip next 3 sts, Fan in next st, skip next 3 sts; rep from * to end, work end st.

Step 12 Using B, rep step 2.

Steps 13–20 Using A, rep steps 3–4.

Step 21 Using B, skip 1st vertical bar, *skip next 3 sts, Fan in next st, skip next 3 sts, 1 Tss in next 7 sts; rep from * to end, work end st.

Step 22 Using B, rep step 2.

Step 23 Rep steps 3–22, changing color as set.

This large fan pattern works well in two or more colors, and is ideal for garments and home accessories. Change color on the return pass when two loops are left on the hook; finish off the pass with the new color.

28 Fan Waves

This bold stitch works well in two or more colors. It is perfect for large pieces such as blankets and wraps. Change color on the return pass when two loops are left on the hook; finish off the pass with the new color.

Special stitches Fan: Inserting hook as for Tks, work 5 Tdc in same st.

Half Fan: Inserting hook as for Tks, work 3 Tdc in same st.

Use colors as follows:
Steps 1–2: A
Steps 3–4: B
Steps 5–6: A
Steps 7–8: C
Steps 9–10: B
Steps 11–12: C
Steps 13–14: A

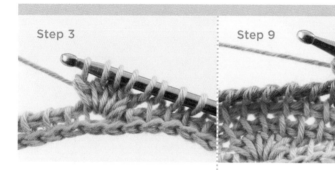

Step 3

Step 9

*skip next 2 sts, Fan in next st, skip next 2 sts, 1 Tss in next 3 sts; rep from * to last 3 sts, skip next 2 sts, Half Fan in next st, work end st.

Steps 11, 13 Rep step 5.

Step 15 Rep steps 3–14, changing color as set.

Multiple 8 sts + 3.

Steps 1–2 Work foundation row (see page 16).

Step 3 Skip 1st vertical bar, 1 Tss in next 2 sts, *skip next 2 sts, Fan in next st, skip next 2 sts, 1 Tss in next 3 sts; rep from * to end, ending last rep with 1 Tss in next 2 sts, work end st.

Steps 4, 6, 8, 10, 12, 14 Rep step 2.

Step 5 Skip 1st vertical bar, 1 Tss in each st to end, work end st.

Step 7 Rep step 5.

Step 9 Skip 1st vertical bar, Half Fan in next st, skip next 2 sts, 1 Tss in next 3 sts,

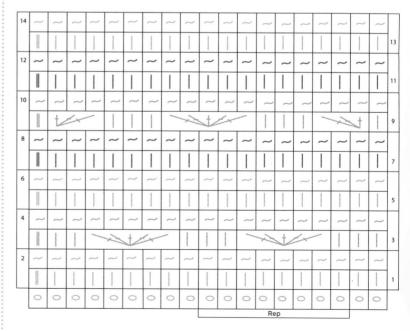

29 V Stitch and Fan

Suitable for many types of projects, this beautiful pattern works up very quickly and looks equally attractive in one color. It is created by first working V stitches, and then filling those stitches with Tunisian double crochet. Change color on the return pass when two loops are left on the hook; finish off the pass with the new color.

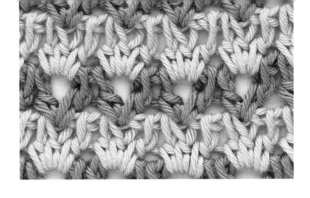

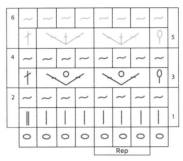

Step 3

Step 5

Step 6

Multiple 3 sts + 2.

Special stitches Double V st: Inserting hook as for Tks, work [1 Tdc, yo, 1 Tdc] in same st.

Fan: Work 3 Tdc in sp at center of V st.

Steps 1–2 Using A, work foundation row (see page 16).

Step 3 Using A, ch 1, skip 1st vertical bar, *skip next st, Double V st in next st, skip next st; rep from * to end, 1 Tdc in end st.

Step 4 Using A, rep step 2.

Step 5 Using B, ch 1, skip 1st vertical bar, *skip next st, Fan in next V st, skip next st; rep from * to end, 1 Tdc in end st.

Step 6 Using B, rep step 2.

Step 7 Rep steps 3–6, changing color as set.

30 Lacy Honeycomb

The small shells are created on the return pass after a row of extended Tunisian simple stitch. This combination produces a fabric with beautiful drape that is ideal for summer garments and accessories. The creation of shells opens up the fabric, making it perfect for shawls and wraps. The pattern could be further emphasized by working rows in different colors.

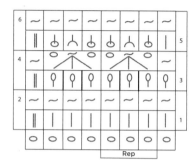

Step 3

Multiple 3 sts + 2.

Special stitch ETss (extended Tunisian simple stitch): Insert hook from right to left under front vertical bar of st, yo and pull through, ch 1.

Steps 1–2 Work foundation row (see page 16).

Step 3 Ch 1, skip 1st vertical bar, 1 ETss in each st to end, work end st.

Step 4

Step 4 Yo and pull through 1 loop on hook, *ch 1, yo and pull through 4 loops (shell made), ch 1; rep from * until 2 loops left on hook, yo and pull through 2 loops.

Step 5

Step 5 Skip 1st vertical bar, *1 Tss in each ch and top of shell to end, work end st.

Step 6 Rep step 2.

Step 7 Rep steps 3–6.

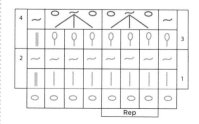

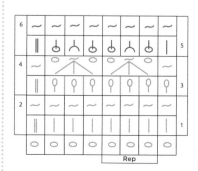

31 Upside-Down Fan

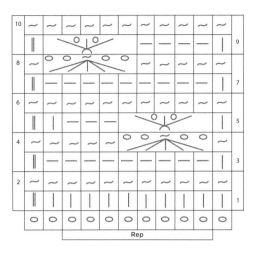

Producing fabric with beautiful drape, this lovely shell stitch is perfect for lacy garments and accessories. When counting stitches off the hook when creating shells, the loop on the hook counts as 1.

Special stitch Arch: Skip 2 ch, [1 Tss, yo, 1 Tss, yo, 1 Tss] in top of shell, skip 2 ch.

Step 3

Step 4

Step 5

Multiple 8 sts + 3.

Steps 1–2 Work foundation row (see page 16).

Step 3 Skip 1st vertical bar, 1 Tps in each st to end, work end st.

Step 4 Yo and pull through 1 loop on hook, yo and pull through 2 loops, *[yo and pull through 2 loops] 3 times, ch 2, yo and pull through 6 loops (shell made), ch 2; rep from * until 2 loops left

on hook, yo and pull through 2 loops.

Step 5 Skip 1st vertical bar, *Arch, 1 Tps in next 3 sts; rep from * to last st, 1 Tss in next st, work end st.

Step 6 Rep step 2.

Step 7 Rep step 3.

Step 8 Yo and pull through 1 loop on hook, *ch 2, yo and pull through 6 loops (shell made), ch 2, [yo and

pull through 2 loops] 3 times; rep from * until 3 loops left on hook, [yo and pull through 2 loops] twice.

Step 9 Skip 1st vertical bar, 1 Tps in next st, *1 Tps in next 3 sts, Arch; rep from * to end, work end st.

Step 10 Rep step 2.

Step 11 Rep steps 3–10.

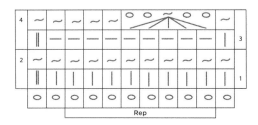

32 Cluster Stitch

This stitch is the perfect introduction to creating clusters in Tunisian crochet. The clusters are made by working three double crochets together in the same place. The key here is to pull tighter on the Tunisian simple stitches on either side of the cluster; this will result in the cluster pulling down and being more prominent. You might need to push the clusters to the front of the fabric. This stitch produces a dense fabric with fair drape, making it perfect for accessories and homewares.

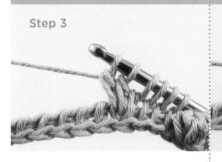

Step 3 | **Step 3 (cont.)** | **Step 7**

Multiple 4 sts + 3.

Special stitch CL (cluster)—Tdc3tog (Tunisian double crochet 3 together): [yo, insert hook as for Tks, yo and pull through, yo and pull through 2 loops on hook] 3 times in same st, yo and pull through 3 loops.

Steps 1–2 Work foundation row (see page 16).

Step 3 Skip 1st vertical bar, 1 Tss in next 2 sts, *CL in next st, 1 Tss in next 3 sts; rep from * to end, ending last rep with 1 Tss in next 2 sts, work end st.

Step 4 Rep step 2.

Step 5 Skip 1st vertical bar, 1 Tss in each st to end, work end st.

Step 6 Rep step 2.

Step 7 Skip 1st vertical bar, *CL in next st, 1 Tss in next 3 sts; rep from * to last st, 1 Tss in next st, work end st.

Step 8 Rep steps 2–7, ending with step 2.

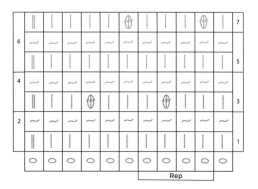

33 Mock Bobble

A fun stitch that gives the fabric lots of texture, the mock bobbles are produced by working chains onto Tunisian simple stitches. It is an easy pattern to memorize and lends itself to homewares such as pillows.

34 Puff Stitch

This stitch is created by working three half double crochets together in the same place. The fabric is ideal for homewares and items that require durability, such as bags and mats.

Step 3	Step 7

Multiple 2 sts + 1.

Steps 1–2 Work foundation row (see page 16).

Step 3 Skip 1st vertical bar, 1 Tss in next st, ch 4, *1 Tss in next 2 sts, ch 4; rep from * to end, work end st.

Step 4 Rep step 2.

Step 5 Skip 1st vertical bar, 1 Tss in each st to end, work end st.

Step 6 Rep step 2.

Step 7 Skip 1st vertical bar, *1 Tss in next 2 sts, ch 4; rep from * to last st, 1 Tss in next st, work end st.

Step 8 Rep steps 2–7, ending with step 2.

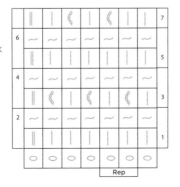

Step 5	Step 5 (cont.)

Multiple 2 sts + 1.

Special stitch Puff—hdc3tog (half double crochet 3 together): [yo, insert hook as for Tks, yo and pull through] 3 times in same st, yo and pull through 6 loops on hook.

Steps 1–2 Work foundation row (see page 16).

Step 3 Skip 1st vertical bar, 1 Tss in next st, *Puff in next st, 1 Tss in next st; rep from * to end, work end st.

Step 4 Rep step 2.

Step 5 Skip 1st vertical bar, Puff in next st, *1 Tss in next st, Puff in next st; rep from * to end, work end st.

Step 6 Rep step 2.

Step 7 Rep steps 3–6.

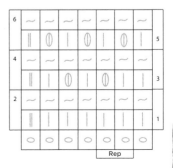

35 Contrasting Puffs

This stitch features big puffs in a contrast color, making them stand out beautifully against the Tunisian simple stitch background. When changing to the contrast color, catch the yarn at the back of a few simple stitches before placing the puff; do this by placing it on top of the working yarn after finishing a Tss. When the next Tss is worked, the contrast yarn will be trapped. Do the same when carrying the contrast yarn between puffs across a row, otherwise the work will pucker. Cut the contrast color after every puff row.

Step 3

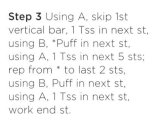

Step 3 (cont.)

Step 7

Multiple 6 sts + 5.

Special stitch Puff—hdc5tog (half double crochet 5 together): [yo, insert hook as for Tks, yo and pull through] 5 times in same st, yo and pull through 10 loops on hook.

Steps 1–2 Using A, work foundation row (see page 16).

Step 3 Using A, skip 1st vertical bar, 1 Tss in next st, using B, *Puff in next st, using A, 1 Tss in next 5 sts; rep from * to last 2 sts, using B, Puff in next st, using A, 1 Tss in next st, work end st.

Step 4 Using A, rep step 2.

Step 5 Using A, skip 1st vertical bar, 1 Tss in each st to end, work end st.

Step 6 Using A, rep step 2.

Step 7 Using A, skip 1st vertical bar, *1 Tss in next 4 sts, using B, Puff in next st, using A, 1 Tss in next st; rep from * to last 3 sts, 1 Tss in next 3 sts, work end st.

Step 8 Rep steps 2–7, ending with step 2.

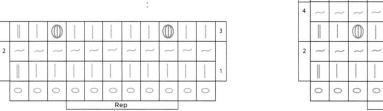

36 Bobbles

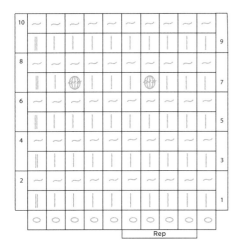

With plenty of texture, this stitch is perfect for blankets and accessories where one side of a project is shown. It looks beautiful in one or more colors. Change color on the return pass when two loops are left on the hook; finish off the pass with the new color. For ease, carry the color not in use up the side of the work and catch it in the second stitch on Tss rows. This will reduce the number of ends to weave in.

Step 7

Step 7 (cont.)

Step 7 (cont.)

Multiple 4 sts + 2.

Special stitch Bobble— Tdc5tog (Tunisian double crochet 5 together): [yo, insert hook as for Tks, yo and pull through, yo and pull through 2 loops on hook] 5 times in same st, yo and pull through 5 loops.

Steps 1–2 Using A (to end of step 10), work foundation row (see page 16).

Step 3 Skip 1st vertical bar, *1 Tss in each st to end, work end st.

Steps 4, 6, 8, 10 Rep step 2.

Step 5 Rep step 3.

Step 7 Skip 1st vertical bar, *1 Tss in next 2 sts, Bobble in next st, 1 Tss in next st; rep from * to end, work end st.

Step 9 Rep step 3.

Step 11 Using B, rep steps 3–10, then continue pattern changing color as set.

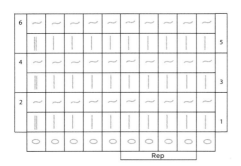

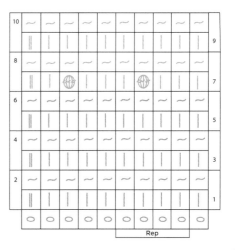

37 Shells and Clusters

This very pretty stitch is easy to work but appears difficult. It is ideal for accessories and garments because the stitch holds its shape well, while also having a lovely, airy feel. When counting stitches off the hook when creating shells, the loop on the hook counts as 1. Change color at the end of the return pass when two loops are left on the hook; finish off the pass with the new color. At the end of the forward pass, complete the end stitch in the current color and then work the first chain of the return pass with the new color.

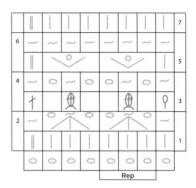

Step 1

Step 2

Step 3

Multiple 3 sts + 2.

Special stitches CL (cluster)—Tdc3tog (Tunisian double crochet 3 together): [yo, insert hook as for Tks, yo and pull through, yo and pull through 2 loops on hook] 3 times in same st, yo and pull through 3 loops.

Simple V st: [1 Tss, yo, 1 Tss] in top of CL.

Step 1 Using A, 1 Tss in 2nd ch from hook and in each ch to end.

Step 2 Using A, yo and pull through 1 loop on hook, *ch 1, yo and pull through 4 loops (shell made), ch 1; rep from * until 2 loops left on hook, yo and pull through 2 loops.

Step 3 Using B, ch 1, skip 1st vertical bar, *skip next ch, CL in top of shell, skip next ch; rep from * to end, 1 Tdc in end st.

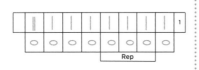
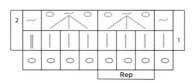
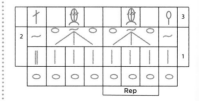

Step 4

Step 5

Step 7

Step 4 Using A, yo and pull through 1 loop on hook, *ch 1, yo and pull through 2 loops, ch 1; rep from * until 2 loops left on hook, yo and pull through 2 loops.

Step 5 Skip 1st vertical bar, *skip next ch, Simple V st in top of CL, skip next ch; rep from * to end, work end st.

Step 6 Yo and pull through 1 loop on hook, *yo and pull through 2 loops; rep from * until 1 loop left on hook.

Step 7 Skip 1st vertical bar, *1 Tss in each st to end, work end st.

Step 8 Rep steps 2–7, changing color as set and ending with step 2.

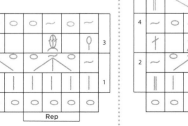

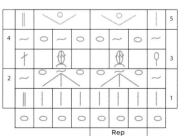

38 Bobble Grid

This is an ideal stitch for homewares and items that need to be durable, such as bags. It looks lovely in lots of colors or just a single color. The bobbles are created by working five double crochets together in the same place. Change color on the return pass when two loops are left on the hook; finish off the pass with the new color.

Multiple 8 sts + 7.

Special stitches Bobble—Tdc5tog (Tunisian double crochet 5 together): [yo, insert hook as for Tks, yo and pull through, yo and pull loop through 2 loops on hook] 5 times in same st, yo and pull through 5 loops.

Long Ttr (long Tunisian treble crochet): Working loosely, [yo] twice, insert hook in top of Bobble 4 rows below, yo and pull through, [yo and pull through 2 loops on hook] twice.

Steps 1–2 Using A, work foundation row (see page 16).

Step 2

Step 3

Step 3 Using B, skip 1st vertical bar, 1 Tss in next 2 sts, *Bobble in next st, 1 Tss in next 7 sts; rep from * to last 3 sts, Bobble in next st, 1 Tss in next 2 sts, work end st.

Step 5

Steps 4, 6, 8 Using B, rep step 2.

Step 5 Using B, skip 1st vertical bar, Bobble in next st, *1 Tss in next 3 sts, Bobble in next st; rep from * to end, work end st.

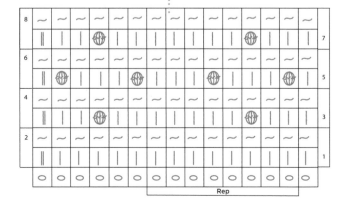

Step 7

Step 14   Step 15

Step 7 Using B, rep step 3.

Step 9 Using A, skip 1st vertical bar, *1 Tss in each st to end, work end st.

Step 10 Using A, rep step 2.

Steps 11–14 Using A, rep steps 9–10.

Step 15 Using B, skip 1st vertical bar, 1 Tss in next 2 sts, *1 Long Ttr, 1 Tss in next 7 sts; rep from * to last 3 sts, 1 Long Ttr, 1 Tss in next 2 sts, work end st.

Step 16 Using B, rep step 2.

Step 17 Rep steps 3–16, changing color as set.

39 Staggered Clusters

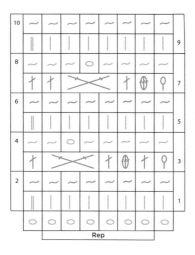

A great stitch combining rows of crossed double crochets and clusters with rows of simple stitch, the fabric is full of texture and interest. It also has no curl, making it perfect for lots of accessories. Change color by working the first chain of the return pass with the new color.

Step 3

Step 7

Step 8

Multiple 6 sts + 2.

Special stitches CL (cluster)—Tdc3tog (Tunisian double crochet 3 together): [yo, insert hook as for Tss, yo and pull through, yo and pull through 2 loops on hook] 3 times in same st, yo and pull through 3 loops.

Crossed Tdc (crossed Tunisian double crochet): Skip next 2 sts, 1 Tdc in next st, 1 Tdc in first skipped st (leave center st unworked).

Steps 1–2 Using A for step 1 and B for step 2, work foundation row (see page 16).

Step 3 Using B, ch 1, skip 1st vertical bar, *1 Tdc in next st, CL in next st, 1 Tdc in next st, Crossed Tdc; rep from * to end, 1 Tdc in end st.

Step 4 Using A, yo and pull through 1 loop on hook, yo and pull through 2 loops, *ch 1, [yo and pull through 2 loops] 5 times; rep from * until 1 loop left on hook.

Step 5 Using A, skip 1st vertical bar, *1 Tss in each st and ch to end, work end st.

Step 6 Using B, rep step 2.

Step 7 Using B, ch 1, skip 1st vertical bar, *CL in next st, 1 Tdc in next st, Crossed Tdc, 1 Tdc in next st; rep from * to end, 1 Tdc in end st.

Step 8 Using A, yo and pull through 1 loop on hook, *[yo and pull through 2 loops] twice, ch 1, [yo and pull through 2 loops] 3 times; rep from * until 2 loops left on hook, yo and pull through 2 loops.

Steps 9–10 Rep steps 5–6.

Step 11 Rep steps 3–10, changing color as set.

40 Cluster Mesh

The soft texture of this stitch makes it ideal for accessories such as scarves and shawls. The fabric also has good drape, perfect for summer garments.

Special stitch CL (cluster)—Tdc2tog (Tunisian double crochet 2 together): [yo, insert hook as for Tks, yo and pull through, yo and pull through 2 loops on hook] twice in same ch or st, yo and pull through 2 loops.

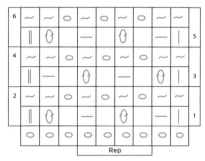

Step 3

Step 4

Multiple 4 sts + 1.

Step 1 1 Tps in 2nd ch from hook, *skip next ch, CL in next ch, skip next ch, 1 Tps in next ch; rep from * to last 3 ch, skip next ch, CL in next ch, 1 Tss in last ch.

Step 2 Yo and pull through 1 loop on hook, *yo and pull through 2 loops, ch 1; rep from * until 3 loops left on hook, [yo and pull through 2 loops] twice.

Step 3 Skip 1st vertical bar, *CL in next st, skip next ch, 1 Tps in next st, skip next ch; rep from * to last 3 sts, CL in next st, skip next ch, 1 Tps in next st, work end st.

Step 4 Rep step 2.

Step 5 Skip 1st vertical bar, 1 Tps in next st, *skip next ch, CL in next st, skip next ch, 1 Tps in next st; rep from * to last 2 sts, skip next ch, CL in next st, work end st.

Step 6 Rep step 2.

Step 7 Rep steps 3–6.

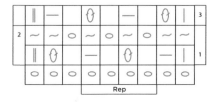

41 Honeycomb Clusters

This dense, highly textured stitch would look great as a section on a scarf or a border on a hat.

Special stitch CL (cluster)—Tdc4tog (Tunisian double crochet 4 together): [yo, insert hook as for Tks, yo and pull through, yo and pull through 2 loops on hook] 4 times in same st, yo and pull through 4 loops.

42 Lozenge

This lovely open stitch is ideal for scarves and wraps. The yarn overs create lots of movement, producing a light, airy fabric.

Special stitch Puff—hdc3tog (half double crochet 3 together): [yo, insert hook as for Tks, yo and pull through] 3 times in same st, yo and pull through 6 loops on hook.

Step 3   Step 7

Step 3   Step 5

Multiple 4 sts + 5.

Steps 1–2 Work foundation row (see page 16).

Step 3 Skip 1st vertical bar, 1 Tks in next st, *CL in next st, 1 Tks in next 3 sts; rep from * to end, ending last rep with 1 Tks in next st, work end st.

Step 4 Rep step 2.

Step 5 Skip 1st vertical bar, *1 Tks in each st to end, work end st.

Step 6 Rep step 2.

Step 7 Skip 1st vertical bar, 1 Tks in next 3 sts, *CL in next st, 1 Tks in next 3 sts; rep from * to end, work end st.

Step 8 Rep steps 2–7, ending with step 2.

Multiple 2 sts + 3.

Steps 1–2 Work foundation row (see page 16).

Step 3 Skip 1st vertical bar, yo, skip next st, *1 Tks in next st, yo, skip next st; rep from * to end, work end st.

Step 4 Rep step 2.

Step 5 Skip 1st vertical bar, skip next st, *Puff in next st, skip next st; rep from * to end, work end st.

Step 6 Yo and pull through 1 loop on hook, *ch 1, yo and

pull through 2 loops; rep from * until 1 loop left on hook.

Step 7 Skip 1st vertical bar, 1 Tss in each ch and st to end, work end st.

Step 8 Rep steps 2–7, ending with step 2.

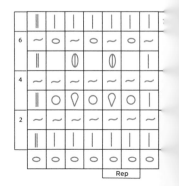

43 Lace Lozenge

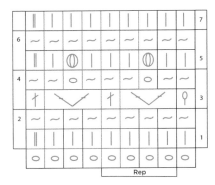

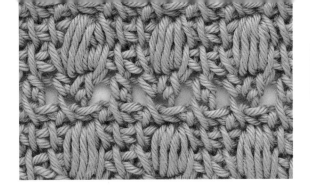

The beautiful open texture in this pattern gives the fabric plenty of drape, making it ideal for garments and shawls. The puffs are set on a background of Tunisian simple stitch, interrupted by rows of lace.

Step 3

Multiple 4 sts + 1.

Special stitch Puff— hdc4tog (half double crochet 4 together): [yo, insert hook as for Tfs, yo and pull through] 4 times in same sp, yo and pull through 8 loops on hook.

Steps 1–2 Work foundation row (see page 16).

Step 3 Ch 1, skip 1st vertical bar, *skip next st, 2 Tdc in next st, skip next st, 1 Tdc in next st; rep from * to end, ending last rep with 1 Tdc in end st.

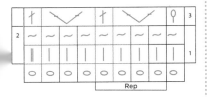

Step 4

Step 4 Yo and pull through 1 loop on hook, yo and pull through 2 loops, *ch 1, [yo and pull through 2 loops] 3 times; rep from * to end, ending last rep with [yo and pull through 2 loops] twice.

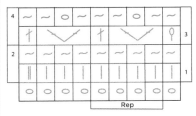

Step 5

Step 5 Skip 1st vertical bar, 1 Tss in next st, Puff in next ch-sp, *1 Tss in next 3 sts, Puff in next ch-sp; rep from * to last st, 1 Tss in next st, work end st.

Step 6 Rep step 2.

Step 7 Skip 1st vertical bar, *1 Tss in each st to end, work end st.

Step 8 Rep steps 2–7, ending with step 2.

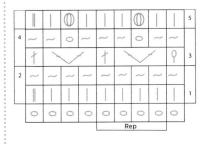

44 Shells and Puffs

This stitch creates a fabric that is bold, textured, and full of interest. It also has good drape, making it suitable for a variety of projects. Experiment with different weights of yarn for different effects. Every row has lots of excitement. Puffs and simple V stitches are created on forward passes, while on return passes the stitches are worked together to create shells. When counting stitches off the hook when creating shells, the loop on the hook counts as 1.

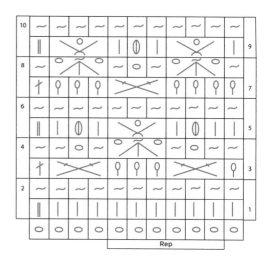

Step 3

Step 7

Multiple 6 sts + 5.

Special stitches Crossed Tdc (crossed Tunisian double crochet): Skip next 2 sts, 1 Tdc in next st, 1 Tdc in first skipped st (leave center st unworked).

ETss (extended Tunisian simple stitch): Insert hook from right to left under front vertical bar of st, yo and pull through, ch 1.

Puff—hdc3tog (half double crochet 3 together): [yo, insert hook as for Tfs, yo and pull through] 3 times in same sp, yo and pull through 6 loops on hook.

Simple V st: [1 Tss, yo, 1 Tss] in top of shell.

Steps 1–2 Work foundation row (see page 16).

Step 3 Ch 1, skip 1st vertical bar, Crossed Tdc, *1 ETss in next 3 sts, Crossed Tdc; rep from * to end, 1 Tdc in end st.

Step 4 Yo and pull through 1 loop on hook, *yo and pull through 2 loops, ch 1, yo and pull through 2 loops, ch 1, yo and pull through 4 loops (shell made), ch 1; rep from * until 4 loops left on hook, yo and pull through 2 loops, ch 1, [yo and pull through 2 loops] twice.

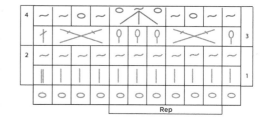

Step 9

Step 8 Yo and pull through 1 loop on hook, ch 1, yo and pull through 4 loops (shell made), ch 1, *[yo and pull through 2 loops, ch 1] twice, yo and pull through 4 loops (shell made), ch 1; rep from * until 2 loops left on hook, yo and pull through 2 loops.

Step 9 Skip 1st vertical bar, skip next ch, Simple V st in top of shell, skip next ch, *1 Tss in next st, Puff in next ch-sp, 1 Tss in next st, skip next ch, Simple V st in top of shell, skip next ch; rep from * to end, work end st.

Step 10 Rep step 2.

Step 11 Rep steps 3–10.

Step 5 Skip 1st vertical bar, 1 Tss in next st, Puff in next ch-sp, 1 Tss in next st, *skip next ch, Simple V st in top of shell, skip next ch, 1 Tss in next st, Puff in next ch-sp, 1 Tss in next st; rep from * to end, work end st.

Step 6 Rep step 2.

Step 7 Ch 1, skip 1st vertical bar, 1 ETss in next 3 sts, *Crossed Tdc, 1 ETss in next 3 sts; rep from * to end, 1 Tdc in end st.

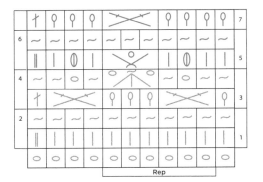

45 Heart Stitch

This sweet stitch lends itself perfectly to bigger projects such as blankets. The fabric has fair drape, and it is best to use a larger hook than recommended for the yarn. The open puffs are worked by gathering yarn wraps onto the hook on the forward pass, and then working them off on the return pass. The stitch count increases on the forward pass, then is reduced on the return pass. When counting stitches off the hook when closing the puffs on the return pass, the loop on the hook counts as 1.

Step 4

Step 5

Multiple 6 sts + 6.

Special stitch OP (open puff): Working loosely, [yo, insert hook in st as for Tks or in ch-sp as for Tfs, yo and pull through] 3 times in same place (6 loops made), leave loops on hook.

Steps 1–2 Work foundation row (see page 16).

Step 3 Skip 1st vertical bar, 1 Tss in next 4 sts, *[OP in next st] twice, 1 Tss in next 4 sts; rep from * to end, work end st.

Step 4 Yo and pull through 1 loop on hook, [yo and pull through 2 loops] 4 times, *yo and pull through 7 loops, ch 1, yo and pull through 7 loops, [yo and pull through 2 loops] 4 times; rep from * until 2 loops left on hook, yo and pull through 2 loops.

Step 5 Skip 1st vertical bar, 1 Tss in next 4 sts, *skip next OP, 2 OP in next ch-sp, skip next OP, 1 Tss in next 4 sts; rep from * to end, work end st.

Step 6 Rep steps 4–5, ending with step 4.

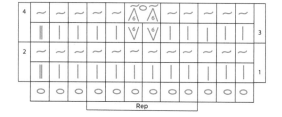

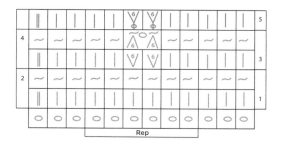

46 Full Heart Stitch

The hearts in this attractive stitch are created from open puffs. These are worked by gathering yarn wraps onto the hook on the forward pass, and then working them off on the return pass. This is a yarn-hungry stitch with very little stretch, but it looks beautiful as a blanket or pillow. It is important to work the open puffs loosely. The stitch count increases on the forward pass, then is reduced on the return pass. When counting stitches off the hook when closing the puffs on the return pass, the loop on the hook counts as 1.

Step 2

Multiple 4 sts + 4.

Special stitch OP (open puff): Working loosely, [yo, insert hook in ch-sp as for Tfs (or into bump at back of ch when working into foundation ch), yo and pull through] 3 times in same place (6 loops made), leave loops on hook.

Step 1 Skip 1st 3 ch, *[OP in next ch] twice, skip next 2 ch; rep from * to last ch, 1 Tss in last ch.

Step 2 Yo and pull through 1 loop on hook, *yo and pull through 7 loops, ch 1, yo and pull through 7 loops; rep from * until 2 loops left on hook, yo and pull through 2 loops.

Step 3

Step 3 Skip 1st vertical bar, *skip next OP, 2 OP in next ch-sp, skip next OP; rep from * to end, work end st.

Step 4 Rep steps 2–3, ending with step 2.

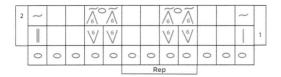

47 Petals

This stunning stitch can be used as a panel to add interest to a plain garment, or in full as a striking wrap. It is an excellent choice for smooth sport-weight yarns. The open puffs are worked in the same way as simple V stitches on the forward pass, and then worked off on the return pass. When counting stitches off the hook when closing the puffs on the return pass, the loop on the hook counts as 1.

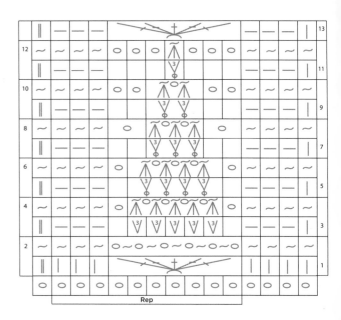

Step 3

Step 4

Step 6

Multiple 10 sts + 5.

Step 1 1 Tss in 2nd ch from hook and in next 2 ch, *skip next 3 ch, Fan in next ch, skip next 3 ch, 1 Tss in next 3 ch; rep from * to last ch, 1 Tss in last ch.

Step 2 Yo and pull through 1 loop on hook, [yo and pull through 2 loops] 3 times, *[ch 1, yo and pull through 2 loops] 6 times, [yo and pull through 2 loops] twice;

rep from * until 2 loops left on hook, yo and pull through 2 loops.

Step 3 Skip 1st vertical bar, 1 Tps in next 3 sts, *skip next ch, [OP in next st, skip next ch] 5 times, 1 Tps in next 3 sts; rep from * to end, work end st.

Step 4 Yo and pull through 1 loop on hook, [yo and pull through 2 loops] 3 times, *ch 1, [yo and pull through 4 loops, ch 1] 5 times, [yo

and pull through 2 loops] 3 times; rep from * until 2 loops left on hook, yo and pull through 2 loops.

Step 5 Skip 1st vertical bar, 1 Tps in next 3 sts, *skip next ch and st, [OP in next ch-sp, skip next st] 4 times, skip next ch, 1 Tps in next 3 sts; rep from * to end, work end st.

Step 6 Yo and pull through 1 loop on hook, [yo and pull through 2 loops] 3 times, *ch 1, [yo and pull through 4 loops, ch 1] 4 times, [yo and pull through 2 loops] 3 times; rep from * until 2 loops left on hook, yo and pull through 2 loops.

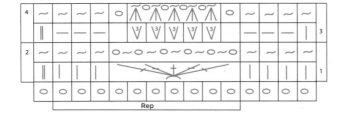

Special stitches Fan: Inserting hook in top of open puff (or into bump at back of ch when working into foundation ch), work 5 Tdc in same place.

OP (open puff): Working loosely, insert hook in st as for Tks or in ch-sp as for Tfs, yo and pull through, yo, insert hook in same st or sp, yo and pull through (3 loops made), leave loops on hook.

Step 7	Step 11	Step 13

Step 7 Skip 1st vertical bar, 1 Tps in next 3 sts, *skip next ch and st, [OP in next ch-sp, skip next st] 3 times, skip next ch, 1 Tps in next 3 sts; rep from * to end, work end st.

Step 8 Yo and pull through 1 loop on hook, [yo and pull through 2 loops] 3 times, *ch 1, [yo and pull through 4 loops, ch 1] 3 times, [yo and pull through 2 loops] 3 times; rep from * until 2 loops left on hook, yo and pull through 2 loops.

Step 9 Skip 1st vertical bar, 1 Tps in next 3 sts, *skip next ch and st, [OP in next ch-sp, skip next st] twice, skip next ch, 1 Tps in next 3 sts; rep from * to end, work end st.

Step 10 Yo and pull through 1 loop on hook, [yo and pull through 2 loops] 3 times, *ch 2, yo and pull through 4 loops, ch 1, yo and pull through 4 loops, ch 2, [yo and pull through 2 loops] 3 times; rep from * until 2 loops left on hook, yo and pull through 2 loops.

Step 11 Skip 1st vertical bar, 1 Tps in next 3 sts, *skip next 2 ch and st, OP in next ch-sp, skip next st and 2 ch, 1 Tps in next 3 sts; rep from * to end, work end st.

Step 12 Yo and pull through 1 loop on hook, [yo and pull through 2 loops] 3 times, *ch 3, yo and pull through 4 loops, ch 3, [yo and pull through 2 loops] 3 times; rep from * until 2 loops left

on hook, yo and pull through 2 loops.

Step 13 Skip 1st vertical bar, 1 Tps in next 3 sts, *skip next 3 ch, Fan in next OP, skip next 3 ch, 1 Tps in next 3 sts; rep from * to end, work end st.

Step 14 Rep steps 2–13, ending with step 12. After final rep of step 12, work 1 Tss in each st, back bar of OP, and back bar of ch to end, then work a return pass followed by a row of standard crochet slip stitch.

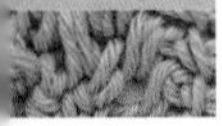

48 Small Petals

Small petals worked on a background of Tunisian simple stitch are perfect as a panel on garments or as an edging on blankets. The open puffs are worked in the same way as simple V stitches on the forward pass, and then worked off on the return pass. When counting stitches off the hook when closing the puffs on the return pass, the loop on the hook counts as 1.

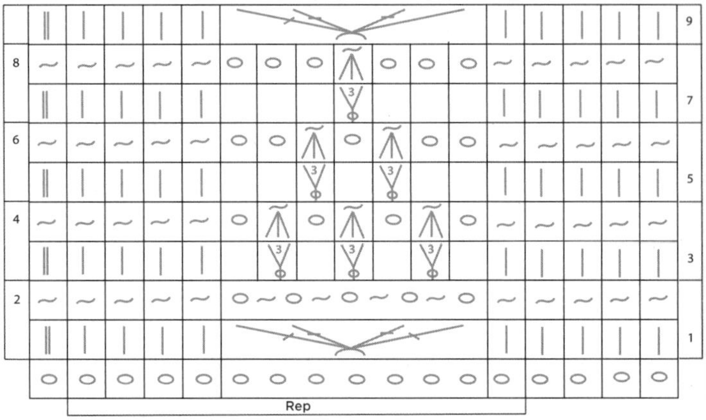

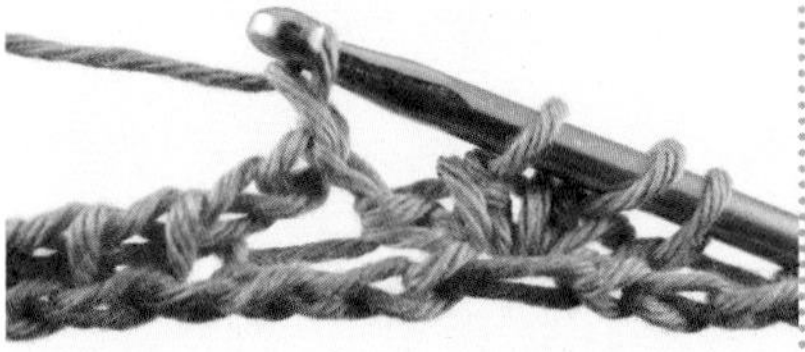

Step 2

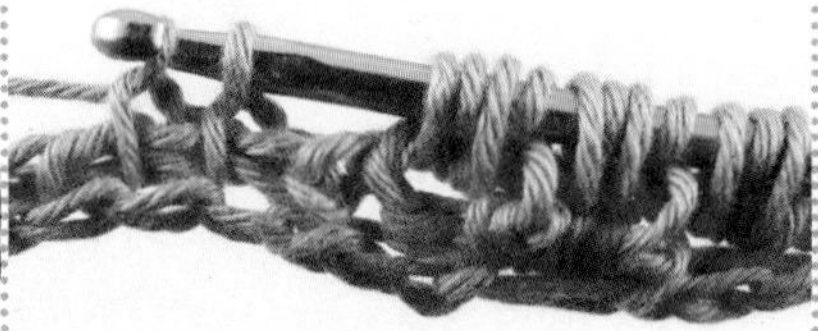

Step 3

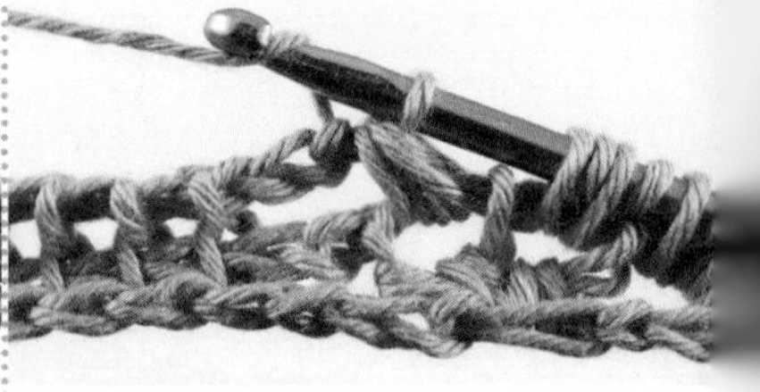

Step 4

Multiple 12 sts + 5.

Step 1 1 Tss in 2nd ch from hook and in next 3 ch, *skip next 3 ch, Fan in next ch, skip next 3 ch, 1 Tss in next 5 ch; rep from * to end.

Step 2 Yo and pull through 1 loop on hook, [yo and pull through 2 loops] 4 times, *[ch 1, yo and pull through 2 loops] 5 times, [yo and pull through 2 loops] 4 times; rep from * until 1 loop left on hook.

Step 3 Skip 1st vertical bar, 1 Tss in next 4 sts, *skip next ch and st, [OP in next ch-sp, skip next st] 3 times, skip next ch, 1 Tss in next 5 sts; rep from * to end, ending last rep with 1 Tss in next 4 sts, work end st.

Step 4 Yo and pull through 1 loop on hook, [yo and pull through 2 loops] 4 times, *ch 1, [yo and pull through 4 loops, ch 1] 3 times, [yo and pull through 2 loops] 5 times; rep from * until 1 loop left on hook.

Step 5 Skip 1st vertical bar, 1 Tss in next 4 sts, *skip next ch and st, [OP in next ch-sp, skip next st] twice, skip next ch, 1 Tss in next 5 sts; rep from * to end, ending last rep with 1 Tss in next 4 sts, work end st.

Step 6 Yo and pull through 1 loop on hook, [yo and pull through 2 loops] 4 times, *ch 2, yo and pull through 4 loops, ch 1, yo and pull through 4 loops, ch 2, [yo and pull through 2 loops] 5 times; rep from * until 1 loop left on hook.

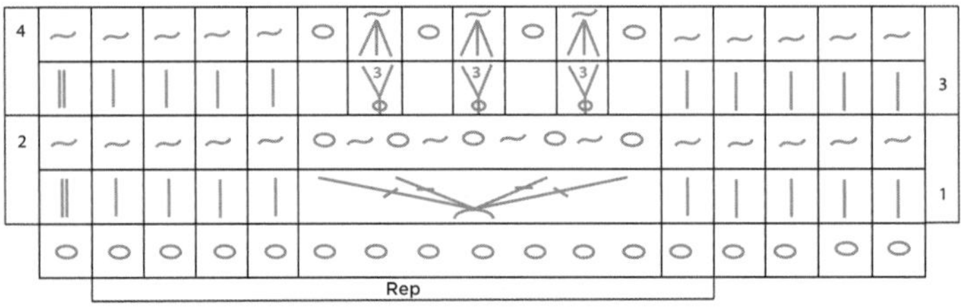

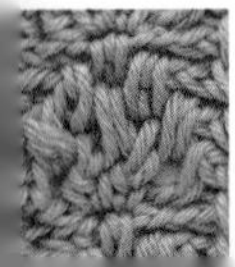

Special stitches Fan: Inserting hook in top of open puff (or into bump at back of ch when working into foundation ch), work 4 Tdc in same place.

OP (open puff): Working loosely, insert hook in ch-sp as for Tfs, yo and pull through, yo, insert hook in same sp, yo and pull through (3 loops made), leave loops on hook.

Step 7

Step 8

Step 9

Step 7 Skip 1st vertical bar, 1 Tss in next 4 sts, *skip next 2 ch and st, OP in next ch-sp, skip next st and 2 ch, 1 Tss in next 5 sts; rep from * to end, ending last rep with 1 Tss in next 4 sts, work end st.

Step 8 Yo and pull through 1 loop on hook, [yo and pull through 2 loops] 4 times, *ch 3, yo and pull through 4 loops, ch 3, [yo and pull through 2 loops] 5 times; rep from * until 1 loop left on hook.

Step 9 Skip 1st vertical bar, 1 Tss in next 4 sts, *skip next 3 ch, Fan in next OP, skip next 3 ch, 1 Tss in next 5 sts; rep from * to end, ending last rep with 1 Tss in next 4 sts, work end st.

Step 10 Rep steps 2-9, ending with step 8. After final rep of step 8, work 1 Tss in each st, back bar of OP, and back bar of ch to end, then work a return pass followed by a row of standard crochet slip stitch.

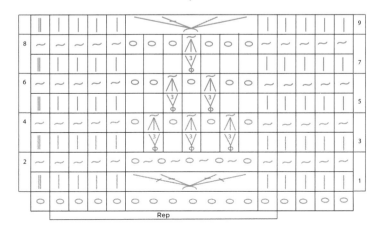

49 Star Stitch

This gorgeous stitch looks best in smooth yarns, and will look wonderful as a panel on a cardigan. Creating the star requires some concentration at first, but the finished effect is very rewarding. The stars are set on a background of Tunisian simple stitch, producing a fabric with fair drape. They are made by working a decrease followed immediately by an increase to return to the original number of stitches. The stars result in the fabric pulling in, causing some tightness.

Step 7

Step 7 (cont.)

Multiple 9 sts + 4.

Special stitch Tss5tog Star (Tunisian simple stitch 5 together star): Insert hook under next 5 front vertical bars at same time, yo and pull through, [yo, insert hook through same 5 bars, yo and pull through] twice (5 new loops on hook).

Steps 1–2 Work foundation row (see page 16).

Step 3 Skip 1st vertical bar, 1 Tss in each st to end, work end st.

Steps 4, 6, 8, 10, 12 Rep step 2.

Step 5 Rep step 3.

Step 7 Skip 1st vertical bar, 1 Tss in next 3 sts, *Tss5tog Star, 1 Tss in next 4 sts; rep from * to end, ending last rep with 1 Tss in next 3 sts, work end st.

Steps 9, 11 Rep step 3.

Step 13 Rep steps 5–12.

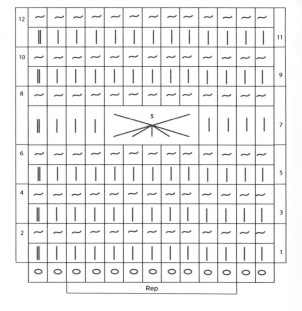

50 Staggered Stars

Stars placed close together on a background of Tunisian purl and simple stitch result in a fabric full of texture and interest. The star stitches cause the fabric to tighten, so it is advisable to use a larger hook than recommended for the yarn. The stars are made by working a decrease followed immediately by an increase to return to the original number of stitches.

Special stitch Tss5tog Star (Tunisian simple stitch 5 together star): Insert hook under next 5 front vertical bars at same time, yo and pull through, [yo, insert hook through same 5 bars, yo and pull through] twice (5 new loops on hook).

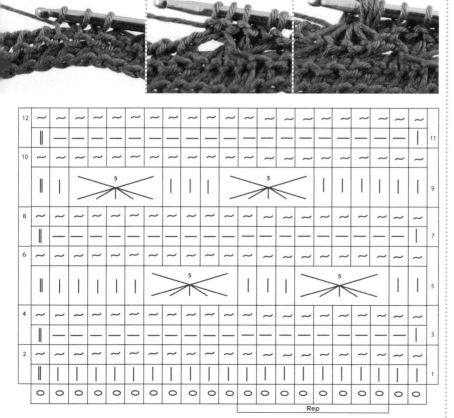

Step 5   Step 7   Step 9

Multiple 8 sts + 5.

Steps 1–2 Work foundation row (see page 16).

Step 3 Skip 1st vertical bar, 1 Tps in each st to end, work end st.

Steps 4, 6, 8, 10, 12 Rep step 2.

Step 5 Skip 1st vertical bar, 1 Tss in next st, *Tss5tog Star, 1 Tss in next 3 sts; rep from * to last 2 sts, 1 Tss in next 2 sts, work end st.

Step 7 Rep step 3.

Step 9 Skip 1st vertical bar, 1 Tss in next 5 sts, Tss5tog Star, *1 Tss in next 3 sts, Tss5tog Star; rep from * to last st, 1 Tss in next st, work end st.

Step 11 Rep step 3.

Step 13 Rep steps 5–12.

51 Tiny Stars

Tiny stars produce fabric with good drape, perfect for garments and accessories.

Special stitch Tss3tog Star (Tunisian simple stitch 3 together star): Insert hook under next 3 front vertical bars at same time, yo and pull through, yo, insert hook through same 3 bars, yo and pull through (3 new loops on hook).

52 Puff Galore

Easy to memorize, this stitch produces fabric with good drape, perfect for garments and accessories.

Special stitch Puff—hdc2tog (half double crochet 2 together): [yo, insert hook as for Tks, yo and pull through] twice in same st, yo and pull through 4 loops on hook.

Step 3 | Step 3 (cont.)

Step 2 | Step 3

Multiple 3 sts + 2.

Steps 1–2 Work foundation row (see page 16).

Step 3 Skip 1st vertical bar, *Tss3tog Star; rep from * to end, work end st.

Step 4 Rep step 2.

Step 5 Skip 1st vertical bar, 1 Tss in each st to end, work end st.

Step 6 Rep step 2.

Step 7 Rep steps 3–6.

Multiple 2 sts.

Changing color
Work first chain of return pass with new color.

Steps 1–2 Using A for step 1 and B for step 2, work foundation row (see page 16).

Step 3 Using B, skip 1st vertical bar, *Puff in next st, 1 Tss in next st; rep from * to end, work end st.

Step 4 Using A, rep step 2.

Step 5 Using A, skip 1st vertical bar, *1 Tss in next st, Puff in next st; rep from * to end, work end st.

Step 6 Using B, rep step 2.

Step 7 Rep steps 3–6, changing color as set.

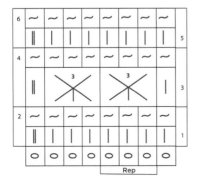

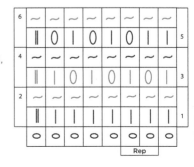

53 Puff Openwork

A playful stitch that is ideal for any project, this pattern will look great in any number of yarn and color combinations. The puffs are made by working two half double crochets together into chain spaces. Change color by working the first chain of the return pass with the new color.

Step 3

Step 5

Multiple 2 sts + 2.

Special stitches Tss2tog (Tunisian simple stitch 2 together): Insert hook under next 2 front vertical bars at same time, yo and pull through.

Puff—hdc2tog (half double crochet 2 together): [yo, insert hook as for Tfs, yo and pull through] twice in same sp, yo and pull through 4 loops on hook.

Steps 1–2 Using A for step 1 and B for step 2, work foundation row (see page 16).

Step 3 Using B, skip 1st vertical bar, *Tss2tog; rep from * to end, work end st.

Step 4 Using A, yo and pull through 1 loop on hook, *ch 1, yo and pull through 2 loops; rep from * until 2 loops left on hook, yo and pull through 2 loops.

Step 5 Using A, skip 1st vertical bar, *1 Tps in next st, Puff in next ch-sp; rep from * to end, work end st.

Step 6 Using B, rep step 2.

Step 7 Rep steps 3–6, changing color as set.

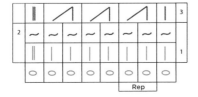

54 Front Clusters

Easy to memorize, this interesting stitch has plenty of texture and lends itself to homewares such as pillows and blankets. The clusters are created by working two double crochets together into the vertical bar of a stitch a few rows below.

Special stitch Long CL (long cluster)—Tdc2tog (Tunisian double crochet 2 together): Working into next st 3 rows below, [yo, insert hook as for Tss, yo and pull through, yo and pull through 2 loops on hook] twice in same st, yo and pull through 2 loops.

Step 17	Step 17 (cont.)

Multiple 4 sts + 7.

Steps 1–2 Work foundation row (see page 16).

Step 3 Skip 1st vertical bar, 1 Tss in each st to end, work end st.

Steps 4, 6, 8, 10, 12, 14, 16, 18 Rep step 2.

Steps 5, 7 Rep step 3.

Step 9 Skip 1st vertical bar, 1 Tss in next 4 sts, *Long CL, 1 Tss in next 3 sts; rep from * to end, ending last rep with 1 Tss in next 4 sts, work end st.

Steps 11, 13, 15 Rep step 3.

Step 17 Skip 1st vertical bar, 1 Tss in next 2 sts, *Long CL, 1 Tss in next 3 sts; rep from * to end, ending last rep with 1 Tss in next 2 sts, work end st.

Step 19 Rep step 3.

Step 20 Rep steps 4–19, ending with step 4.

55 Claw

This fun stitch has plenty of texture and visual interest. The claws are worked in a contrast color, but the stitch would look just as good in one color. When changing to the contrast color, catch the yarn at the back of a few simple stitches before placing the claw; do this by placing it on top of the working yarn after finishing a Tss. When the next Tss is worked, the contrast yarn will be trapped. Do the same when carrying the contrast yarn between claws across a row, otherwise the work will pucker. Finish the last stage of the claw in the background color, and cut the contrast color after every claw row.

Special stitch Claw—Ttr3tog (Tunisian treble crochet 3 together): Using B and starting in st 3 rows below Tss just worked, *[yo] twice, insert hook as for Tss, yo and pull through, [yo and pull through 2 loops on hook] twice; rep from * in next st 4 rows below, then rep once more in next st 3 rows below; using A, yo and pull through 3 loops on hook; skip Tss directly below center st of Claw and continue as directed.

Step 19

Step 19 (cont.)

Multiple 6 sts + 1.

Steps 1–2 Using A for background throughout, work foundation row (see page 16).

Step 3 Skip 1st vertical bar, 1 Tss in each st to end, work end st.

Steps 4, 6, 8, 10, 12, 14, 16, 18, 20 Rep step 2.

Steps 5, 7 Rep step 3.

Step 9 Skip 1st vertical bar, 1 Tss in next 2 sts, *Claw, 1 Tss in next 5 sts;

rep from * to end, ending last rep with 1 Tss in next 2 sts, work end st.

Steps 11, 13, 15, 17 Rep step 3.

Step 19 Skip 1st vertical bar, 1 Tss in next 5 sts, *Claw, 1 Tss in next 5 sts; rep from * to end, work end st.

Step 21 Rep step 3.

Step 22 Rep steps 2–21, ending with step 2.

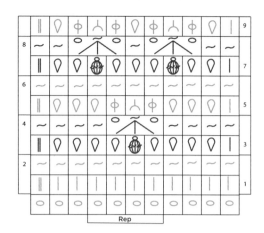

56 Popcorn

The popcorns provide a striking 3D effect and result in a fabric full of movement, perfect for garments, accessories, and homewares. The popcorns are created on the forward pass; the last loop of the popcorn is pulled through the first stitch and secured with a chain.

Special stitch Pc (popcorn)—5 Tdc in same st: Yo, insert hook as for Tks, yo and pull through, yo and pull through 2 loops on hook, [yo, insert hook in same st, yo and pull through, (yo and pull through 2 loops) twice] 4 times, withdraw hook from loop, insert hook in top of first of these 5 Tdc, catch empty loop and pull through, ch 1.

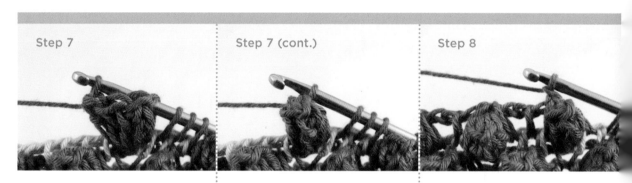

| Step 7 | Step 7 (cont.) | Step 8 |

Multiple 4 sts + 7.

Changing color Change color on return pass when 2 loops left on hook; finish off pass with new color. Use A for steps 1–2 and B for steps 3–4, then alternate two steps in A and two steps in B throughout.

Steps 1–2 Work foundation row (see page 16).

Step 3 Skip 1st vertical bar, 1 Tks in next 4 sts, *Pc in next st, 1 Tks in next 3 sts; rep from * to last st, 1 Tks in next st, work end st.

Step 4 Yo and pull through 1 loop on hook, *[yo and pull through 2 loops] 3 times, *ch 1, yo and pull through

4 loops (shell made), ch 1, yo and pull through 2 loops; rep from * until 4 loops left on hook, [yo and pull through 2 loops] 3 times.

Step 5 Skip 1st vertical bar, 1 Tks in next 3 sts, *1 Tfs in next ch-sp, 1 Tss in top of shell, 1 Tfs in next ch-sp, 1 Tks in next st; rep from to last 2 sts, 1 Tks in next 2 sts, work end st.

Step 6 Rep step 2.

Step 7 Skip 1st vertical bar, 1 Tks in next 2 sts, Pc in next st, *1 Tks in next 3 sts, Pc in next st; rep from * to last 2 sts, 1 Tks in next 2 sts, work end st.

Step 8 Yo and pull through 1 loop on hook, yo and pull through 2 loops, *ch 1, yo and pull through 4 loops (shell made), ch 1, yo and pull through 2 loops; rep from * until 2 loops left on hook, yo and pull through 2 loops.

Step 9 Skip 1st vertical bar, 1 Tks in next st, *1 Tfs in next ch-sp, 1 Tss in top of shell, 1 Tfs in next ch-sp, 1 Tks in next st; rep from to end, work end st.

Step 10 Rep steps 2–9, changing color as set and ending with step 2.

57 Diamond Popcorn

The popcorns stand out on a stripy contrast background, perfect for projects where one side is shown. The popcorns are created on the forward pass; the last loop of the popcorn is pulled through the first stitch and secured with a chain.

Step 5

Step 5 (cont.)

Step 6

Multiple 6 sts + 3.

Special stitch Pc (popcorn)—5 Tdc in same st: Yo, insert hook as for Tks, yo and pull through, yo and pull through 2 loops on hook, [yo, insert hook in same st, yo and pull through, (yo and pull through 2 loops) twice] 4 times, withdraw hook from loop, insert hook in top of first of these 5 Tdc, catch empty loop and pull through, ch 1.

Changing color Change color on return pass when 2 loops left on hook; finish off pass with new color. Use A for steps 1–4 and B for steps 5–6, then alternate two steps in A and two steps in B throughout.

Steps 1–2 Work foundation row (see page 16).

Step 3 Skip 1st vertical bar, 1 Tss in each st to end, work end st.

Steps 4, 6, 8, 10, 12, 14, 16, 18 Rep step 2.

Step 5 Skip 1st vertical bar, 1 Tss in next st, *Pc in next st, 1 Tss in next 5 sts; rep from * to end, work end st.

Step 7 Rep step 3.

Step 9 Skip 1st vertical bar, *Pc in next st, 1 Tss in next st, Pc in next st, 1 Tss in next 3 sts; rep from * to last st, Pc in next st, work end st.

Step 11 Rep step 3.

Step 13 Skip 1st vertical bar, 1 Tss in next st, *Pc in next st, 1 Tss in next st; rep from * to end, work end st.

Step 15 Rep step 3.

Step 17 Skip 1st vertical bar, Pc in next st, *1 Tss in next st, Pc in next st, 1 Tss in next 3 sts, Pc in next st; rep from * to end, work end st.

Step 19 Rep steps 3–18, changing color as set and ending with step 4.

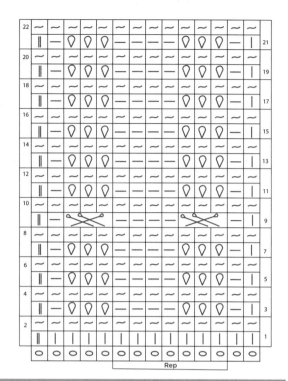

58 Small Twist

This stitch is the perfect introduction to Tunisian crochet cables. The twists are worked using Tunisian knit stitch on a background of purl stitch. This pattern creates quite a dense fabric, making it perfect for winter accessories.

Step 9

Step 9 (cont.)

Step 10

Multiple 7 sts + 7.

Special stitch T3st cable (Tunisian 3 stitch cable): skip next 2 sts, 1 Tks in next st, 1 Tks in 2nd skipped st, 1 Tks in first skipped st.

Steps 1–2 Work foundation row (see page 16).

Step 3 Skip 1st vertical bar, 1 Tps in next st, *1 Tks in next 3 sts, 1 Tps in next 4 sts; rep from * to last 4 sts, 1 Tks in next 3 sts, 1 Tps in next st, work end st.

Step 4 Rep step 2.

Steps 5–8 Rep steps 3–4.

Step 9 Skip 1st vertical bar, 1 Tps in next st, *T3st cable, 1 Tps in next 4 sts; rep from * to last 4 sts, T3st cable, 1 Tps in next st, work end st.

Step 10 Rep step 2.

Steps 11–22 Rep steps 3–4.

Step 23 Rep steps 9–22.

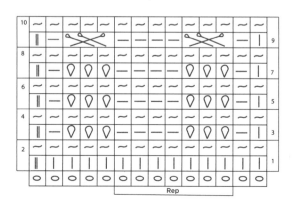

59 Basic Cable

This sweet stitch is worked in a similar way to knitted cables. The cables are worked in Tunisian simple stitch with columns of purl stitch in between. The cables look great placed together or individually as an accent. You will need a cable needle.

Step 9	Step 9 (cont.)	Step 16

Multiple 5 sts + 3.

Special stitch C4F (cable 4 front): Slip front vertical bars of next 2 sts onto cable needle and hold at front of work, 1.Tss in next 2 sts, 1 Tss in each st on cable needle.

Steps 1–2 Work foundation row (see page 16).

Step 3 Skip 1st vertical bar, 1 Tps in next st, *1 Tss in next 4 sts, 1 Tps in next st; rep from * to end, work end st.

Step 4 Rep step 2.

Steps 5–8 Rep steps 3–4.

Step 9 Skip 1st vertical bar, 1 Tps in next st, *C4F, 1 Tps in next st; rep from * to end, work end st.

Step 10 Rep step 2.

Steps 11–16 Rep steps 3–4.

Step 17 Rep steps 9–16.

60 Antler

Made by working cables in opposite directions, the finished pattern mimics the antlers of a stag. The stitch looks beautiful as a single panel and is perfect for adding interest to cardigans and sweaters. The fabric is quite firm and pulls in a lot, so take this into account on projects where size is important. You will need a cable needle.

(chart rows 1–16, with "Rep" marked at base)

Step 5

Multiple 14 sts + 3.

Special stitches C6B (cable 6 back): Slip front vertical bars of next 3 sts onto cable needle and hold at back of work, 1 Tss in next 3 sts, 1 Tss in each st on cable needle.

C6F (cable 6 front): Slip front vertical bars of next 3 sts onto cable needle and hold at front of work, 1 Tss in next 3 sts, 1 Tss in each st on cable needle.

Step 7

Steps 1–2 Work foundation row (see page 16).

Step 3 Skip 1st vertical bar, 1 Tps in next st, *1 Tss in next 6 sts, 1 Tps in next st; rep from * to end, work end st.

Step 4 Rep step 2.

Step 7 (cont.)

Steps 5–6 Rep steps 3–4.

Step 7 Skip 1st vertical bar, 1 Tps in next st, *C6B, 1 Tps in next st, C6F, 1 Tps in next st; rep from * to end, work end st.

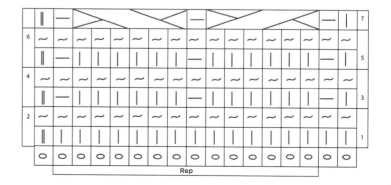

(chart rows 1–7, with "Rep" marked at base)

Step 7 (cont.)

Step 8

Step 9

Step 8 Rep step 2.

Steps 9–16 Rep steps 3–4.

Step 17 Rep steps 7–16.

61 Garlic Braid

This beautiful cable is perfect as a panel with smaller cable stitches on either side. The pattern is worked in Tunisian simple stitch on a background of purl stitch to make the cable prominent. The front and back cables are worked in line to make a striking design. You will need a cable needle.

Step 5

Step 5 (cont.)

Step 6

Multiple 13 sts + 6.

Special stitches C6F (cable 6 front): Slip front vertical bars of next 3 sts onto cable needle and hold at front of work, 1 Tss in next 3 sts, 1 Tss in each st on cable needle.

C6B (cable 6 back): Slip front vertical bars of next 3 sts onto cable needle and hold at back of work, 1 Tss in next 3 sts, 1 Tss in each st on cable needle.

Steps 1–2 Work foundation row (see page 16).

Step 3 Skip 1st vertical bar, 1 Tps in next 4 sts, *1 Tss in next 9 sts, 1 Tps in next 4 sts; rep from * to end, work end st.

Step 4 Rep step 2.

Step 5 Skip 1st vertical bar, 1 Tps in next 4 sts, *1 Tss in next 3 sts, C6F, 1 Tps in next 4 sts; rep from * to end, work end st.

Step 6 Rep step 2.

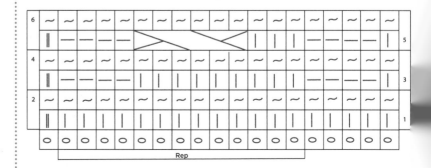

Step 13

Step 13 (cont.)

Step 15

Steps 7–12 Rep steps 3–4.

Step 13 Skip 1st vertical bar, 1 Tps in next 4 sts, *C6B, 1 Tss in next 3 sts, 1 Tps in next 4 sts; rep from * to end, work end st.

Step 14 Rep step 2.

Steps 15–18 Rep steps 3–4.

Step 19 Rep steps 3–18.

62 Pinched

This playful stitch will look beautiful on a large project such as a blanket where the design has lots of space to shine. The cables are spread out on a Tunisian simple stitch background, making the fabric drape nicely. You will need a cable needle.

Step 5	Step 5 (cont.)	Step 18

Multiple 12 sts + 4.

Special stitches C4B (cable 4 back): Slip front vertical bars of next 2 sts onto cable needle and hold at back of work, 1 Tss in next 2 sts, 1 Tss in each st on cable needle.

C4F (cable 4 front): Slip front vertical bars of next 2 sts onto cable needle and hold at front of work, 1 Tss in next 2 sts, 1 Tss in each st on cable needle.

Steps 1–2 Work foundation row (see page 16).

Step 3 Skip 1st vertical bar, 1 Tss in each st to end, work end st.

Step 4 Rep step 2.

Step 5 Skip 1st vertical bar, 1 Tss in next st, *C4B, 1 Tss in next 4 sts, C4F; rep from * to last st, 1 Tss in next st, work end st.

Step 6 Rep step 2.

Steps 7–12 Rep steps 3–4.

Step 13 Skip 1st vertical bar, 1 Tss in next 3 sts, *C4F, C4B, 1 Tss in next 4 sts; rep from * to end, ending last rep with 1 Tss in next 3 sts, work end st.

Step 14 Rep step 2.

Steps 15–18 Rep steps 3–4.

Step 19 Rep steps 3–18.

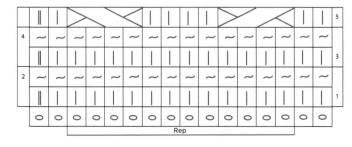

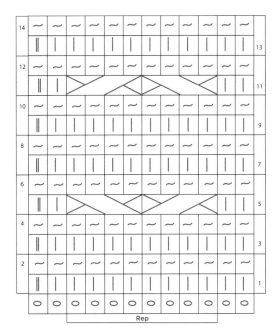

63 Honeycomb Cable

The front and back cables are placed next to each other to create a striking honeycomb pattern. This stitch is quite dense and produces a fabric with little drape. You will need a cable needle.

Step 5

Step 5 (cont.)

Step 11

Multiple 8 sts + 4.

Special stitches C4B (cable 4 back): Slip front vertical bars of next 2 sts onto cable needle and hold at back of work, 1 Tss in next 2 sts, 1 Tss in each st on cable needle.

C4F (cable 4 front): Slip front vertical bars of next 2 sts onto cable needle and hold at front of work, 1 Tss in next 2 sts, 1 Tss in each st on cable needle.

Steps 1–2 Work foundation row (see page 16).

Step 3 Skip 1st vertical bar, 1 Tss in each st to end, work end st.

Step 4 Rep step 2.

Step 5 Skip 1st vertical bar, 1 Tss in next st, *C4B, C4F; rep from * to last st, 1 Tss in next st, work end st.

Step 6 Rep step 2.

Steps 7–10 Rep steps 3–4.

Step 11 Skip 1st vertical bar, 1 Tss in next st, *C4F, C4B; rep from * to last st, 1 Tss in next st, work end st.

Step 12 Rep step 2.

Steps 13–14 Rep steps 3–4

Step 15 Rep steps 3–14.

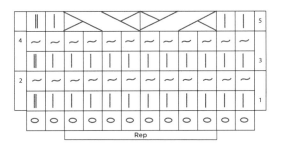

64 Garden Path

The front and back cables are staggered to create a very interesting design. This stitch works perfectly as a single column or in a group. You will need a cable needle.

Special stitches C4F (cable 4 front): Slip front vertical bars of next 2 sts onto cable needle and hold at front of work, 1 Tss in next 2 sts, 1 Tss in each st on cable needle.

C4B (cable 4 back): Slip front vertical bars of next 2 sts onto cable needle and hold at back of work, 1 Tss in next 2 sts, 1 Tss in each st on cable needle.

Step 3	Step 9	Step 11

Multiple 8 sts + 4.

Steps 1–2 Work foundation row (see page 16).

Step 3 Skip 1st vertical bar, 1 Tps in next 2 sts, *1 Tss in next 2 sts, C4F, 1 Tps in next 2 sts; rep from * to end, work end st.

Step 4 Rep step 2.

Step 5 Skip 1st vertical bar, 1 Tps in next 2 sts, *1 Tss in next 6 sts, 1 Tps in next 2 sts; rep from * to end, work end st.

Step 6 Rep step 2.

Steps 7–10 Rep steps 5–6.

Step 11 Skip 1st vertical bar, 1 Tps in next 2 sts, *1 Tss in next 2 sts, C4F, 1 Tps in next 2 sts; rep from * to end, work end st.

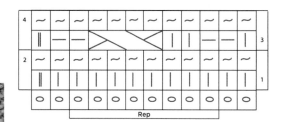

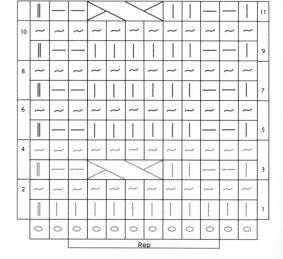

Step 15

Step 12 Rep step 2.

Steps 13–14 Rep steps 5–6

Step 15 Skip 1st vertical bar, 1 Tps in next 2 sts, *C4B, 1 Tss in next 2 sts, 1 Tps in next 2 sts; rep from * to end, work end st.

Step 16 Rep step 2.

Steps 17–22 Rep steps 5–6.

Step 23 Skip 1st vertical bar, 1 Tps in next 2 sts, *C4B, 1 Tss in next 2 sts, 1 Tps in next 2 sts; rep from * to end, work end st.

Step 24 Rep step 2.

Steps 25–26 Rep steps 5–6.

Step 27 Rep steps 3–26.

65 Lattice

Stunning to look at and interesting to work, this stitch is perfect for a large range of projects from garments to blankets. Front and back cables and added twists create the beautiful lattice design. The twists are worked over four stitches using a combination of Tunisian simple and purl stitches. You will need a cable needle.

Special stitches C4B (cable 4 back): Slip front vertical bars of next 2 sts onto cable needle and hold at back of work, 1 Tss in next 2 sts, 1 Tss in each st on cable needle.

C4F (cable 4 front): Slip front vertical bars of next 2 sts onto cable needle and hold at front of work, 1 Tss in next 2 sts, 1 Tss in each st on cable needle.

T4B (twist 4 back): Slip front vertical bars of next 2 sts onto cable needle and hold at back of work, 1 Tss in next 2 sts, 1 Tps in each st on cable needle.

T4F (twist 4 front): Slip front vertical bars of next 2 sts onto cable needle and hold at front of work, 1 Tps in next 2 sts, 1 Tss in each st on cable needle.

Step 3

Multiple 8 sts + 12.

Steps 1–2 Work foundation row (see page 16).

Step 3 Skip 1st vertical bar, 1 Tps in next 3 sts, C4B, *1 Tps in next 4 sts, C4B; rep from * to last 3 sts, 1 Tps in next 3 sts, work end st.

Step 4 Rep step 2.

Step 5 Skip 1st vertical bar, 1 Tps in next 3 sts, *1 Tss in next 4 sts, 1 Tps in next 4 sts; rep from * to end, ending last rep with 1 Tps in next 3 sts, work end st.

Step 6 Rep step 2.

Step 7

Step 7 Skip 1st vertical bar, 1 Tps in next st, *T4B, T4F; rep from * to last st, 1 Tps in next st, work end st.

Step 8 Rep step 2.

Step 7 (cont.)

Step 9 Skip 1st vertical bar, 1 Tps in next st, 1 Tss in next 2 sts, 1 Tps in next 4 sts, *1 Tss in next 4 sts, 1 Tps in next 4 sts; rep from * to last 3 sts, 1 Tss in next 2 sts, 1 Tps in next st, work end st.

Step 10 Rep step 2.

Step 11

Step 11 Skip 1st vertical bar, 1 Tps in next st, 1 Tss in next 2 sts, 1 Tps in next 4 sts, *C4F, 1 Tps in next 4 sts; rep from * to last 3 sts, 1 Tps in next 2 sts, 1 Tps in next st, work end st.

Step 12 Rep step 2.

Steps 13–14 Rep steps 9–10.

Step 15 Skip 1st vertical bar, 1 Tps in next st, *T4F, T4B; rep from * to last st, 1 Tps in next st, work end st.

Step 16 Rep step 2.

Steps 17–18 Rep steps 5–6.

Step 19 Rep steps 3–18.

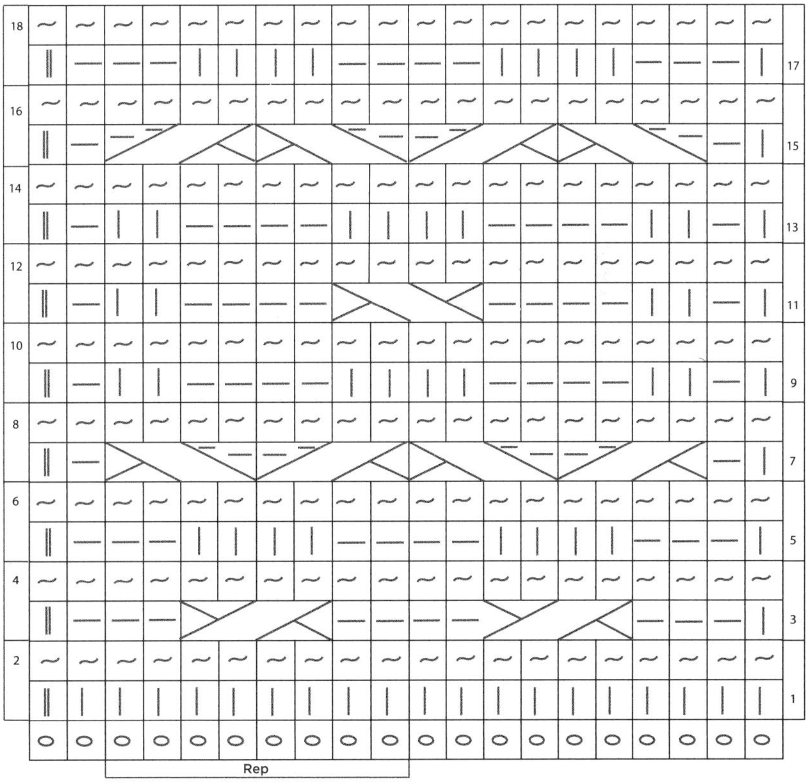

66 Linked Ovals

A simple but effective design, this stitch is perfect as a single column or in groups. The ovals are created by twists worked over three stitches; the ovals are joined at top and bottom by front and back cables. You will need a cable needle.

Special stitches C4B (cable 4 back): Slip front vertical bars of next 2 sts onto cable needle and hold at back of work, 1 Tss in next 2 sts, 1 Tss in each st on cable needle.

C4F (cable 4 front): Slip front vertical bar of next 2 sts onto cable needle and hold at front of work, 1 Tss in next 2 sts, 1 Tss in each st on cable needle.

T3B (twist 3 back): Slip front vertical bar of next st onto cable needle and hold at back of work, 1 Tss in next 2 sts, 1 Tps in st on cable needle.

T3F (twist 3 front): Slip front vertical bars of next 2 sts onto cable needle and hold at front of work, 1 Tps in next st, 1 Tss in each st on cable needle.

Step 7

Step 7 (cont.)

Step 7 (cont.)

Multiple 10 sts + 4.

Steps 1–2 Work foundation row (see page 16).

Step 3 Skip 1st vertical bar, 1 Tps in next st, *1 Tps in next 3 sts, C4B, 1 Tps in next 3 sts; rep from * to last st, 1 Tps in next st, work end st.

Step 4 Rep step 2.

Step 5 Skip 1st vertical bar, 1 Tps in next st, *1 Tps in next 3 sts, 1 Tss in next 4 sts, 1 Tps in next 3 sts; rep from * to last st, 1 Tps in next st, work end st.

Step 6 Rep step 2.

Step 7 Skip 1st vertical bar, 1 Tps in next st, *1 Tps in next 2 sts, T3B, T3F, 1 Tps in next 2 sts, rep from * to last st, 1 Tps in next st, work end st.

Step 8 Rep step 2.

Step 9 Skip 1st vertical bar, 1 Tps in next st, *1 Tps in next 2 sts, [1 Tss in next 2 sts, 1 Tps in next 2 sts] twice; rep from * to last st, 1 Tps in next st, work end st.

Step 10 Rep step 2.

Step 11 Skip 1st vertical bar, 1 Tps in next st, *1 Tps in next st, T3B, 1 Tps in next 2 sts, T3F, 1 Tps in next st; rep from * to last st, 1 Tps in next st, work end st.

Step 12 Rep step 2.

Step 13 Skip 1st vertical bar, 1 Tps in next st, *1 Tps in next st, 1 Tss in next 2 sts, 1 Tps in next 4 sts, 1 Tss in next 2 sts, 1 Tps in next st; rep from * to last st, 1 Tps in next st, work end st.

Step 14 Rep step 2.

Steps 15–18 Rep steps 13–14.

Step 19 Skip 1st vertical bar, 1 Tps in next st, *1 Tps in next st, T3F, 1 Tps in next 2 sts, T3B, 1 Tps in next st; rep from * to last st, 1 Tps in next st, work end st.

Step 20 Rep step 2.

Step 19

Step 21 Skip 1st vertical bar, 1 Tps in next st, *1 Tps in next 2 sts, [1 Tss in next 2 sts, 1 Tps in next 2 sts] twice; rep from * to last st, 1 Tps in next st, work end st.

Step 22 Rep step 2.

Step 23 Skip 1st vertical bar, 1 Tps in next st, *1 Tps in next 2 sts, T3F, T3B, 1 Tps in next 2 sts; rep from * to last st, 1 Tps in next st, work end st.

Step 24 Rep step 2.

Step 25 Skip 1st vertical bar, 1 Tps in next st, *1 Tps in next 3 sts, 1 Tss in next 4 sts, 1 Tps in next 3 sts; rep from * to last st, 1 Tps in next st, work end st.

Step 26 Rep step 2.

Step 27 Rep steps 3–26.

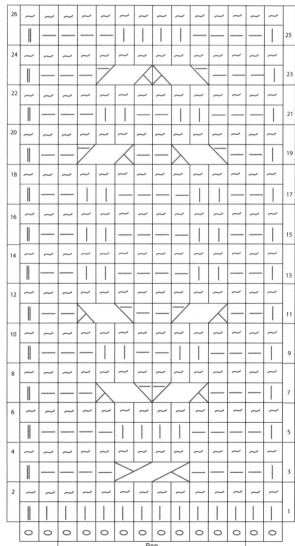

67 Basketweave I

There are many variations of basketweave stitch. This one is worked in alternating blocks of six Tunisian simple and purl stitches, resulting in fabric with more drape than basketweaves worked over smaller blocks. This stitch lends itself perfectly to projects such as blankets and accessories.

Step 12

Step 13

Step 13 (cont.)

Multiple 12 sts + 12.

Steps 1–2 Work foundation row (see page 16).

Step 3 Skip 1st vertical bar, 1 Tss in next 5 sts, *1 Tps in next 6 sts, 1 Tss in next 6 sts; rep from * to last 5 sts, 1 Tps in next 5 sts, work end st.

Step 4 Rep step 2.

Steps 5–12 Rep steps 3–4.

Step 13 Skip 1st vertical bar, 1 Tps in next 5 sts, *1 Tss in next 6 sts, 1 Tps in next 6 sts; rep from * to last 5 sts, 1 Tss in next 5 sts, work end st.

Step 14 Rep step 2.

Steps 15–22 Rep steps 13–14.

Step 23 Rep steps 3–22.

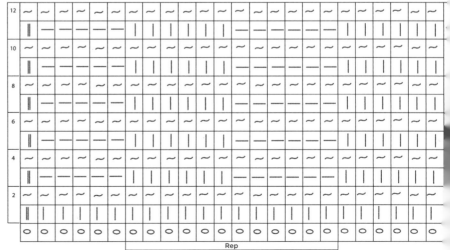

22																								
20																								21
18																								19
16																								17
14																								15
12																								13
10																								11
8																								9
6																								7
4																								5
2																								3
																								1

Rep

68 Basketweave II

This combination of Tunisian knit and purl stitches produces fabric with good stability and drape. The pattern is perfect for several kinds of projects, including winter garments, blankets, and accessories.

Step 7

Step 7 (cont.)

Step 8

Multiple 8 sts + 8.

Steps 1–2 Work foundation row (see page 16).

Step 3 Skip 1st vertical bar, 1 Tks in next 3 sts, *1 Tps in next 4 sts, 1 Tks in next 4 sts; rep from * to last 3 sts, 1 Tps in next 3 sts, work end st.

Step 4 Rep step 2.

Steps 5–8 Rep steps 3–4.

Step 9 Skip 1st vertical bar, 1 Tps in next 3 sts, *1 Tks in next 4 sts, 1 Tps in next 4 sts; rep from * to last 3 sts, 1 Tks in next 3 sts, work end st.

Step 10 Rep step 2.

Steps 11–14 Rep steps 9–10.

Step 15 Rep steps 3–14.

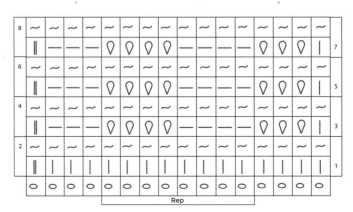

69 Crossed

The crossed stitches are created by skipping a stitch, working Tunisian simple stitch in the next stitch and then working simple stitch in the skipped stitch.

70 Crossed Doubles

Crossed Tunisian double crochets make an attractive textured fabric that is suitable for a large number of projects, such as garments and homewares.

Step 3	Step 4

Multiple 2 sts + 2.

Special stitch
Crossed Tss (crossed Tunisian simple stitch): Skip next st, 1 Tss in next st, 1 Tss in skipped st.

Steps 1–2 Work foundation row (see page 16).

Step 3 Skip 1st vertical bar, *Crossed Tss; rep from * to end, work end st.

Step 4 Rep step 2.

Step 5 Rep steps 3–4.

Step 3	Step 4

Multiple 3 sts + 2.

Special stitch
Crossed Tdc (crossed Tunisian double crochet): Skip next 2 sts, 1 Tdc in next st, 1 Tdc in first skipped st (leave center st unworked).

Steps 1–2 Work foundation row (see page 16).

Step 3 Skip 1st vertical bar, *Crossed Tdc; rep from * to end, work end st.

Step 4 Yo and pull through 1 loop on hook, yo and pull through 2 loops, *ch 1, [yo and pull through 2 loops] twice; rep from * until 1 loop left on hook.

Step 5 Rep steps 3–4.

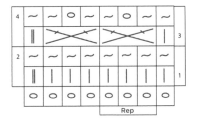

71 Diagonal Cross

This fun stitch is created from diagonal lines of crossed simple stitches. The fabric has fair drape and suits winter accessories such as scarves and hats perfectly.

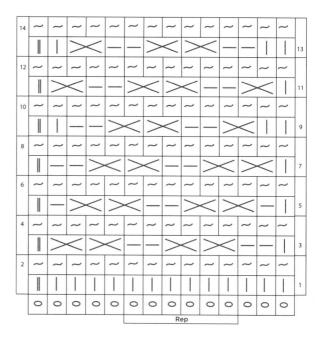

Step 3

Step 5

Multiple 6 sts + 2.

Special stitch Crossed Tss (crossed Tunisian simple stitch): Skip next st, 1 Tss in next st, 1 Tss in skipped st.

Steps 1–2 Work foundation row (see page 16).

Step 3 Skip 1st vertical bar, *1 Tps in next 2 sts, [Crossed Tss] twice; rep from * to end, work end st.

Step 4 Rep step 2.

Step 5 Skip 1st vertical bar, *1 Tps in next st, [Crossed Tss] twice, 1 Tps in next st; rep from * to end, work end st.

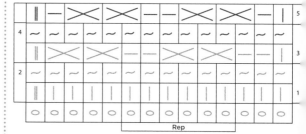

Step 6

Step 6 Rep step 2.

Step 7 Skip 1st vertical bar, *[Crossed Tss] twice, 1 Tps in next 2 sts; rep from * to end, work end st.

Step 8 Rep step 2.

Step 9 Skip 1st vertical bar, 1 Tss in next st, Crossed Tss, *1 Tps in next 2 sts, [Crossed Tss] twice; rep from * to last 3 sts, 1 Tps in next 2 sts, 1 Tss in next st, work end st.

Step 10 Rep step 2.

Step 11 Skip 1st vertical bar, Crossed Tss, 1 Tps in next 2 sts, *[Crossed Tss] twice, 1 Tps in next 2 sts; rep from * to last 2 sts, Crossed Tss, work end st.

Step 12 Rep step 2.

Step 13 Skip 1st vertical bar, 1 Tss in next st, 1 Tps in next 2 sts, *[Crossed Tss] twice, 1 Tps in next 2 sts; rep from * to last 3 sts, Crossed Tss, 1 Tss in next st, work end st.

Step 14 Rep step 2.

Step 15 Rep steps 3–14.

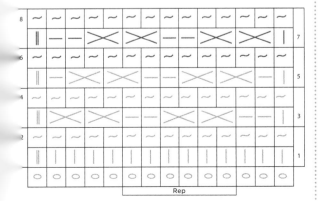

72 Smock

This beautiful stitch lends itself perfectly to many projects. Visually it resembles honeycomb stitch, but it is worked very differently. When working a yarn under, it is paramount that you keep the yarn in place with your index finger the entire time. If the yarn slips, you will create a purl stitch rather than a yarn under.

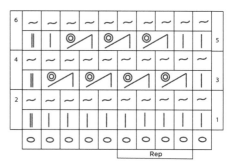

Step 3

Step 3 (cont.)

Multiple 4 sts + 2.

Special stitches Tss2tog (Tunisian simple stitch 2 together): Insert hook under next 2 front vertical bars at same time, yo and pull through.

Yu (yarn under): Bring yarn under hook to front and then wrap it over hook to back (opposite direction from a yarn over); hold wrapped yarn in place on hook with index finger so it does not slip until next st is completed.

Steps 1–2 Work foundation row (see page 16).

Step 3 Skip 1st vertical bar, *Tss2tog, yu; rep from * to end, work end st.

Step 4 Rep step 2.

Step 5 Skip 1st vertical bar, 1 Tss in next st, *Tss2tog, yu; rep from * to last st, 1 Tss in next st, work end st.

Step 6 Rep step 2

Step 7 Rep steps 3–6.

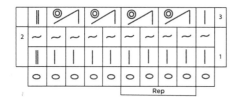

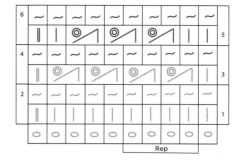

73 Ocean

Full of texture, this stitch would look equally beautiful worked in a combination of colors. It is not an easy stitch and takes a while to master, especially the long Tunisian simple stitches. The first row of long stitches are worked into the foundation chains, and from then on into the top of the shells two rows below.

Special stitch Long Tss (long Tunisian simple stitch): Insert hook in top of shell 2 rows below (or into top leg of ch when working into foundation ch), yo and pull through.

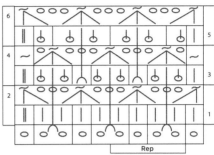

Step 2

Multiple 4 sts + 2.

Step 1 1 Tss in 2nd ch from hook and in each ch to end.

Step 2 Yo and pull through 1 loop on hook, yo and pull through 2 loops (shell made), ch 3, *yo and pull through 4 loops (shell made), ch 3; rep from * until 3 loops left on hook, yo and pull through 3 loops (shell made).

Step 3

Step 3 Skip 1st vertical bar and shell, *1 Tss in next ch, 1 Long Tss in foundation ch between shells, 1 Tss in next ch, skip next shell; rep from * to end, work end st.

Step 4 Yo and pull through 1 loop on hook, ch 1, yo and pull through 4 loops (shell made), *ch 3, yo and pull through 4 loops (shell made); rep from * until 2 loops left on hook, ch 1, yo and pull through 2 loops.

Step 5

Step 5 Skip 1st vertical bar, 1 Tss in next ch, skip next shell, *1 Tss in next ch, 1 Long Tss in top of shell 2 rows below, 1 Tss in next ch, skip next shell; rep from * to last ch, 1 Tss in next ch, work end st.

Step 6 Rep step 2.

Step 7 Rep steps 3–6.

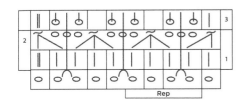

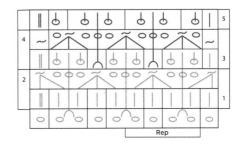

74 Trellis

The subtle use of star stitches results in an uncomplicated pattern but with lots of interest. Using a bigger hook than recommended for the yarn will produce fabric that is ideal for a wide range of projects from homewares to accessories.

Step 5

Step 5 (cont.)

Step 9

Multiple 6 sts + 2.

Special stitch Tss3tog Star (Tunisian simple stitch 3 together star): Insert hook under next 3 front vertical bars at same time, yo and pull through, yo, insert hook through same 3 bars, yo and pull through (3 new loops on hook).

Steps 1–2 Work foundation row (see page 16).

Step 3 Skip 1st vertical bar, 1 Tss in each st to end, work end st.

Step 4 Rep step 2.

Step 5 Skip 1st vertical bar, *1 Tss in next 3 sts, Tss3tog Star; rep from * to end, work end st.

Step 6 Rep step 2.

Steps 7–10 Rep steps 3–4.

Step 11 Skip 1st vertical bar, *Tss3tog Star, 1 Tss in next 3 sts; rep from * to end, work end st.

Step 12 Rep step 2.

Steps 13–14 Rep steps 3–4.

Step 15 Rep steps 3–14.

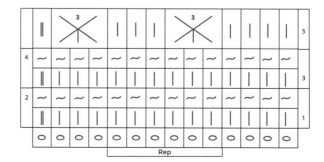

75 Diamonds

Rows of star stitch in alternating colors produce a stripy fabric with little drape and curl, perfect for blankets and scarves. Change color on the return pass when two loops are left on the hook; finish off the pass with the new color. Carry the unused yarn up the side of the work.

76 Sparkle

Worked in three colors, this stitch looks like firework sparklers. The stars are alternated with rows of purl stitch to produce fabric with good drape. Change color by working the first chain of the return pass with the new color. Carry the unused yarn up the side of the work and use it when needed.

Step 3

Step 6

Step 5

Step 7

Multiple 4 sts + 5.

Special stitch
As left.

Steps 1–2 Using A, work foundation row (see page 16).

Step 3 Using B, skip 1st vertical bar, *Tss3tog Star, 1 Tss in next st; rep from * to last 3 sts, Tss3tog Star, work end st.

Step 4 Using B, rep step 2.

Step 5 Using A, skip 1st vertical bar, 1 Tss in next 2 sts,

*Tss3tog Star, 1 Tss in next st; rep from * to last st, 1 Tss in next st, work end st.

Step 6 Using A, rep step 2.

Step 7 Rep steps 3–6, changing color as set.

Multiple 3 sts + 2.

Special stitch
As left.

Steps 1–2 Using A for step 1 and B for step 2, work foundation row (see page 16).

Step 3 Using B, skip 1st vertical bar, 1 Tps in each st to end, work end st.

Step 4 Using C, rep step 2.

Step 5 Using C, skip 1st vertical bar, *Tss3tog Star; rep from * to end, work end st.

Step 6 Using A, rep step 2.

Step 7 Using A, rep step 3.

Step 8 Rep steps 2–7, changing color as set and ending with step 2.

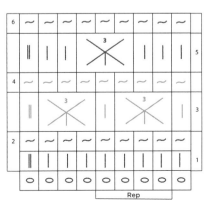

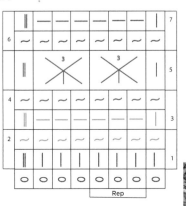

77 Twists and Crosses

This stitch creates a firm fabric that is ideal for homewares. Work it on a much larger hook than recommended for the yarn to give it more movement. Change color by working the first chain of the return pass with the new color. Carry the unused yarn up the side of the work.

78 Bow

This sweet stitch is perfect for adding a little texture to any project. Because the stitch is worked mostly in Tunisian knit stitch with occasional rows of crossed stitch, the fabric will curl a lot. Fix this by using a larger hook than recommended for the yarn, or work an edging around it.

| Step 3 | Step 4 | Step 5 | Step 11 |

Multiple 2 sts + 2.

Special stitches
Crossed Tss (crossed Tunisian simple stitch): Skip next st, 1 Tss in next st, 1 Tss in skipped st.

TwTks (twisted Tunisian knit stitch): Using tip of hook, pull front vertical bar of st to right to reveal back vertical bar, insert hook from front to back through center of st between vertical bars, yo and pull through.

Steps 1–2 Using A for step 1 and B for step 2, work foundation row (see page 16).

Step 3 Using B, skip 1st vertical bar, *Crossed Tss; rep from * to end, work end st.

Step 4 Using A, rep step 2.

Step 5 Using A, skip 1st vertical bar, *1 Tks in next st, 1 TwTks in next st; rep from * to end, work end st.

Step 6 Using B, rep step 2.

Step 7 Rep steps 3–6, changing color as set.

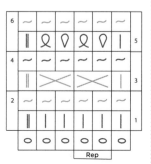

Multiple 2 sts + 2.

Special stitch Crossed Tss (crossed Tunisian simple stitch): Skip next st, 1 Tss in next st, 1 Tss in skipped st.

Steps 1–2 Work foundation row (see page 16).

Step 3 Skip 1st vertical bar, 1 Tks in each st to end, work end st.

Step 4 Rep step 2.

Steps 5–10 Rep steps 3–4.

Step 11 Skip 1st vertical bar, *Crossed Tss; rep from * to end, work end st.

Step 12 Rep step 2.

Step 13 Rep steps 3–12.

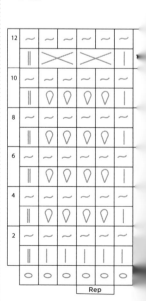

79 Woven

Alternating rows of Tunisian full and knit stitch create a beautiful fabric with good drape. The pattern uses two colors to add visual interest. Change color on the return pass when two loops are left on the hook; finish off the pass with the new color. Carry the unused yarn up the side of the work and use it when needed.

Step 7

Step 9

Multiple 2 sts + 2.

Steps 1–2 Using A, work foundation row (see page 16).

Step 3 Using B, skip 1st vertical bar, 1 Tfs in sp between 1st and 2nd sts, 1 Tfs in each sp to last sp, skip next sp, work end st.

Step 4 Using B, rep step 2.

Step 5 Using A, skip 1st vertical bar, 1 Tks in each st to end, work end st.

Step 6 Using A, rep step 2.

Step 7 Using B, skip 1st vertical bar and sp, 1 Tfs in sp between 2nd and 3rd sts, 1 Tfs in each sp to end, work end st.

Step 8 Using B, rep step 2.

Steps 9–10 Using A, rep steps 5–6.

Step 11 Rep steps 3–10, changing color as set.

80 Checkered

This pattern uses two colors to add texture and interest, but will look equally appealing in one color. It is created by working two stitches together followed by a full stitch to keep the stitch count correct on one row. Tunisian simple and purl stitches are combined on alternating rows to produce an attractive fabric with good drape. Change color by working the first chain of the return pass with the new color. Carry the unused yarn up the side of the work and use it when needed.

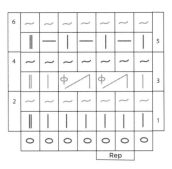

Step 3

Step 3 (cont.)

Multiple 2 sts + 3.

Special stitch Tss2tog (Tunisian simple stitch 2 together): Insert hook under next 2 front vertical bars at same time, yo and pull through.

Steps 1–2 Using A for step 1 and B for step 2, work foundation row (see page 16).

Step 3 Using B, skip 1st vertical bar, *Tss2tog, 1 Tfs in next sp; rep from * to last st, 1 Tss in next st, work end st.

Step 4 Using A, rep step 2.

Step 5 Using A, skip 1st vertical bar, 1 Tps in next st, *1 Tss in next st, 1 Tps in next st; rep from * to end, work end st.

Step 6 Using B, rep step 2.

Step 7 Rep steps 3–6, changing color as set.

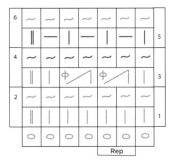

81 Peaks

Perfect for adding simple texture to any project, this stitch will work in any combination of colors. The peaks are made by working two simple stitches together followed by a simple stitch worked into the upper bar of the next stitch to keep the stitch count correct.

82 Texture

This stitch produces fabric with very good drape. It leans to the right, but good blocking will fix this issue. Change color on the return pass when two loops are left on the hook; finish off the pass with the new color. Carry the unused yarn up the side of the work and use it when needed.

Step 3	Step 4

Step 5	Step 5 (cont.)

Multiple 2 sts + 2.

Special stitch
Tss2tog (Tunisian simple stitch 2 together): Insert hook under next 2 front vertical bars at same time, yo and pull through.

Steps 1–2 Work foundation row (see page 16).

Step 3 Skip 1st vertical bar, *Tss2tog (to decrease by 1 st), 1 Tss in upper horizontal bar after st just worked (to substitute decreased st); rep from * to end, work end st.

Step 4 Rep step 2.

Step 5 Rep steps 3–4.

Multiple 2 sts + 2.

Special stitch
Tss2tog (Tunisian simple stitch 2 together): Insert hook under next 2 front vertical bars at same time, yo and pull through.

Steps 1–2 Using A, work foundation row (see page 16).

Step 3 Using B, skip 1st vertical bar, *yo, Tss2tog; rep from * to end, work end st.

Step 4 Using B, rep step 2.

Steps 5–6 Using C, rep steps 3–4.

Step 7 Rep steps 3–4, changing color as set.

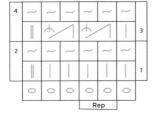

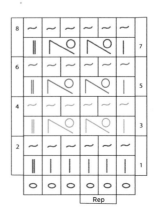

83 Knots

This fun stitch is simple to work but looks more complicated than it is. The fabric has lots of drape and no curling, and can be worked in any number of colors. Change color by working the first chain of the return pass with the new color. Carry the unused yarn up the side of the work.

84 Mock Basketweave

A simple variation of basketweave stitches, this pattern is created with Tunisian double crochets and simple stitch worked over a four-stitch repeat. The fabric has fair drape and lends itself perfectly to any number of projects, from blankets to scarves.

Step 3	Step 6

Step 3	Step 3 (cont.)

Multiple 2 sts + 2.

Steps 1–2 Using A for step 1 and B for step 2, work foundation row (see page 16).

Step 3 Using B, skip 1st vertical bar, *1 Tss in next st, 1 Tdc in next st; rep from * to end, work end st.

Step 4 Using A, rep step 2.

Step 5 Using A, skip 1st vertical bar, *1 Tdc in next st, 1 Tss in next st; rep from * to end, work end st.

Step 6 Using B, rep step 2.

Step 7 Rep steps 3–6, changing color as set.

Multiple 4 sts + 2.

Steps 1–2 Work foundation row (see page 16).

Step 3 Skip 1st vertical bar, *1 Tdc in next 2 sts, 1 Tss in next 2 sts; rep from * to end, work end st.

Step 4 Rep step 2.

Step 5 Skip 1st vertical bar, *1 Tss in next 2 sts, 1 Tdc in next 2 sts; rep from * to end, work end st.

Step 6 Rep step 2.

Step 7 Rep steps 3–6.

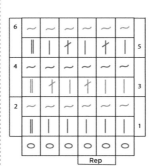

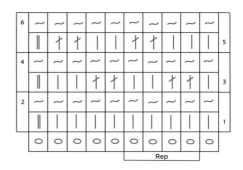

85 Corded

With superb drape and movement, this stitch is perfect for summer garments, accessories, and blankets. Change color on the return pass when two loops are left on the hook; finish off the pass with the new color. Carry the unused yarn up the side of the work and use it when needed.

86 Plow

The vertical lines in this stitch are reminiscent of freshly plowed fields. Tunisian knit stitch is combined with simple stitch worked into the horizontal bars to produce fabric with good drape and interest, perfect for a large variety of projects from homewares to garments.

Step 5	Step 5 (cont.)	Step 3	Step 3 (cont.)

Multiple Any number of sts.

Special stitch ETks (extended Tunisian knit stitch): Insert hook from front to back through center of st between vertical bars, yo and pull through, ch 1.

Steps 1–2 Using A, work foundation row (see page 16).

Step 3 Using B, ch 1, skip 1st vertical bar, 1 ETks in each st to end, 1 Tdc in end st.

Step 4 Using B, rep step 2.

Steps 5–6 Using A, rep steps 3–4.

Step 7 Rep steps 3–6, changing color as set.

Multiple 2 sts + 2.

Steps 1–2 Work foundation row (see page 16).

Step 3 Skip 1st vertical bar, *1 Tks in next st, 1 Tss in

upper and back horizontal bars of next st; rep from * to end, work end st.

Step 4 Rep step 2.

Step 5 Rep steps 3–4.

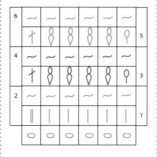

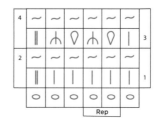

87 Weave

Visually stunning, the combination of Tunisian twisted and simple stitches creates a beautiful pattern. This stitch is quite dense with very little movement, making it suitable for homeware projects such as pillows. Change color by working the first chain of the return pass with the new color. Carry the unused yarn up the side of the work and use it when needed.

Step 3

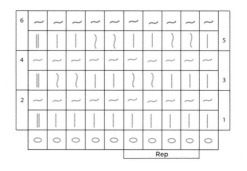

Step 4

Multiple 4 sts + 2.

Special stitch TwTss (twisted Tunisian simple stitch): Using tip of hook, grasp vertical bar of st and twist hook up to right, yo and pull through.

Steps 1–2 Using A for step 1 and B for step 2, work foundation row (see page 16).

Step 3 Using B, skip 1st vertical bar, *1 Tss in next 2 sts, 1 TwTss in next 2 sts; rep from * to end, work end st.

Step 4 Using A, rep step 2.

Step 5 Using A, skip 1st vertical bar, *1 TwTss in next 2 sts, 1 Tss in next 2 sts; rep from * to end, work end st.

Step 6 Using B, rep step 2.

Step 7 Rep steps 3–6, changing color as set.

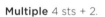

88 Aztec

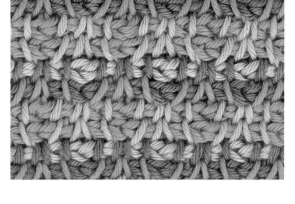

A three-color combination of Tunisian twisted and simple stitch, this dense fabric has a woven look that is ideal for pillows or a winter wrap. The pattern can be worked in any number of colors and is perfect for using up scrap yarn. Change color by working the first chain of the return pass with the new color. Carry the unused yarn up the side of the work and use it when needed.

Step 5

Step 5 (cont.)

Step 7

Multiple 4 sts + 2.

Special stitch TwTss (twisted Tunisian simple stitch): Using tip of hook, grasp vertical bar of st and twist hook up to right, yo and pull through.

Steps 1–2 Using A for step 1 and B for step 2, work foundation row (see page 16).

Step 3 Using B, skip 1st vertical bar, *1 Tss in next 2 sts, 1 TwTss in next 2 sts; rep from * to end, work end st.

Step 4 Using C, rep step 2.

Step 5 Using C, rep step 3.

Step 6 Using A, rep step 2.

Step 7 Using A, skip 1st vertical bar, *1 TwTss in next 2 sts, 1 Tss in next 2 sts; rep from * to end, work end st.

Step 8 Using B, rep step 2.

Step 9 Using B, rep step 7.

Step 10 Using C, rep step 2.

Step 11 Rep steps 3–10 changing color as set.

89 Block

Tunisian post stitches are used to create this attractive stitch with bold texture. The post stitches are worked around both the front and back vertical bars of the stitch below. Combined with purl stitches, the pattern produces a fabric with good drape that will suit a large number of projects, from garments to homewares. Change color on the return pass when two loops are left on the hook; finish off the pass with the new color. Carry the unused yarn up the side of the work and use it when needed.

Step 3

Step 3 (cont.)

Step 4

Multiple 6 sts + 2.

Special stitch Tfpdc (Tunisian front post double crochet): Yo, insert hook from right to left under front and back vertical bars of st, yo and pull through, yo and pull through 2 loops on hook.

Steps 1–2 Using A, work foundation row (see page 16).

Step 3 Using B, skip 1st vertical bar, *1 Tps in next 3 sts, 1 Tfpdc in next 3 sts; rep from * to end, work end st.

Step 4 Using B, rep step 2.

Step 5 Using A, skip 1st vertical bar, *1 Tfpdc in next 3 sts, 1 Tps in next 3 sts; rep from * to end, work end st.

Step 6 Using A, rep step 2.

Step 7 Rep steps 3–6, changing color as set.

90 Brick

Stripes of Tunisian simple stitch are divided into a brick pattern using long front post stitches. The fabric has fair drape and slight curl, which is easily managed by blocking or with a border around the edge. Change color on the return pass when two loops are left on the hook; finish off the pass with the new color. Carry the unused yarn up the side of the work.

Step 5

Step 5 (cont.)

Step 7

Multiple 4 sts + 1.

Special stitch Long Tfpdc (long Tunisian front post double crochet): Yo, insert hook from right to left under front and back vertical bars of next st 2 rows below, yo and pull through, yo and pull through 2 loops on hook.

Steps 1–2 Using A, work foundation row (see page 16).

Step 3 Using B, skip 1st vertical bar, 1 Tss in each st to end, work end st.

Step 4 Using B, rep step 2.

Step 5 Using A, skip 1st vertical bar, 1 Tss in next 3 sts, *1 Long Tfpdc, 1 Tss in next 3 sts; rep from * to end, work end st.

Step 6 Using A, rep step 2.

Steps 7–8 Using B, rep steps 3–4.

Step 9 Using B, skip 1st vertical bar, 1 Tss in next st, *1 Long Tfpdc, 1 Tss in next 3 sts; rep from * to last 2 sts, 1 Long Tfpdc, 1 Tss in next st, work end st.

Step 10 Using A, rep step 4.

Step 11 Rep steps 3–10, changing color as set.

91 Ridged

This boldly textured stitch produces fabric that is quite lacy and airy, ideal for summer garments and accessories. Change color by working the first chain of the return pass with the new color. Carry the unused yarn up the side of the work and use it when needed.

92 Bamboo

The look of bamboo cane is created using wrapped stitches aligned on every row. Use a spare needle to lift the yarn over and place it over the three Tunisian simple stitches to complete each wrap.

Step 3

Step 5

Step 3

Step 3 (cont.)

Multiple 4 sts + 5.

Special stitch
Tss3tog (Tunisian simple stitch 3 together): Insert hook under next 3 front vertical bars at same time, yo and pull through.

Steps 1–2 Using A for step 1 and B for step 2, work foundation row (see page 16).

Step 3 Using B, skip 1st vertical bar, *yo, Tss3tog, yo, 1 Tss in

back horizontal bar of next st; rep from * to last 3 sts, yo, Tss3tog, yo, work end st.

Steps 4–5 Using A, rep steps 2–3.

Step 6 Rep steps 2–5, changing color as set and ending with step 2.

Multiple 3 sts + 2.

Steps 1–2 Work foundation row (see page 16).

Step 3 Skip 1st vertical bar, *yo, 1 Tss in next 3 sts, lift yo loop over last 3 sts and off hook; rep from * to end, work end st.

Step 4 Rep step 2.

Step 5 Rep steps 3–4.

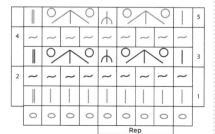

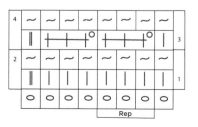

93 Extended Purl

Tunisian purl and extended simple stitches are alternated to create this fun texture. The stitch benefits from being worked in solid-color yarns; multicolored yarns will not showcase the stitch.

94 Small Check

Alternating Tunisian knit and reverse stitches create a beautiful and gentle texture that can be enhanced by working in smooth, solid-color yarns.

Step 3

Step 5

Multiple 2 sts + 2.

Special stitch ETss (extended Tunisian simple stitch): Insert hook from right to left under front vertical bar of st, yo and pull through, ch 1.

Steps 1–2 Work foundation row (see page 16).

Step 3 Skip 1st vertical bar, *1 Tps in next st, 1 ETss in next st; rep from * to end, work end st.

Step 4 Rep step 2.

Step 5 Skip 1st vertical bar, *1 ETss in next st, 1 Tps in next st; rep from * to end, work end st.

Step 6 Rep steps 2–5, ending with row 2.

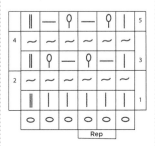

Step 3

Step 5

Multiple 2 sts + 2.

Special stitch Trs (Tunisian reverse stitch): With yarn and hook at back, insert hook from right to left under back vertical bar of st, yo and pull through.

Steps 1–2 Work foundation row (see page 16).

Step 3 Skip 1st vertical bar, *1 Tks in next st, 1 Trs in next st; rep from * to end, work end st.

Step 4 Rep step 2.

Step 5 Skip 1st vertical bar, *1 Trs in next st, 1 Tks in next st; rep from * to end, work end st.

Step 6 Rep steps 2–5, ending with row 2.

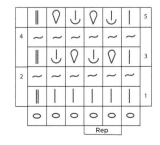

95 Trail

This stitch creates a visually interesting stripe pattern. Use toning colors for a subtle effect or bold ones for a stronger look. Change color on the return pass when two loops are left on the hook; finish off the pass with the new color. Carry the unused yarn up the side of the work and use it when needed.

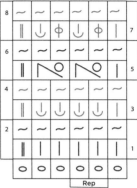

Step 3

Step 5

Step 5 (cont.)

Multiple 2 sts + 2.

Special stitches Trs (Tunisian reverse stitch): With yarn and hook at back, insert hook from right to left under back vertical bar of st, yo and pull through.

Tss2tog (Tunisian simple stitch 2 together): Insert hook under next 2 front vertical bars at same time, yo and pull through.

Steps 1–2 Using A, work foundation row (see page 16).

Step 3 Using B, skip 1st vertical bar, 1 Trs in each st to end, work end st.

Step 4 Using B, rep step 2.

Step 5 Using A, skip 1st vertical bar, *yo, Tss2tog; rep from * to end, work end st.

Step 6 Using A, rep step 2.

Step 7 Using B, skip 1st vertical bar, *1 Tfs in next sp, 1 Trs in next st; repeat from * to end, work end st.

Step 8 Using B, rep step 2.

Step 9 Rep steps 3–8, changing color as set.

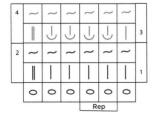

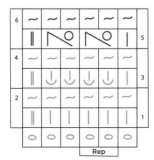

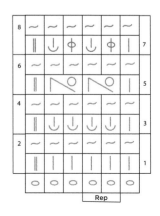

96 Teeth

Tunisian double crochets worked together create stripes of upside-down spikes. Change color by working the first chain of the return pass with the new color. Carry the unused yarn up the side of the work and use it when needed.

97 Rows

This stitch looks subtle in one color, but you can create a bolder look by working stripes in contrasting colors. Tunisian double crochets worked together create a fabric with excellent drape and texture.

| Step 3 | Step 3 (cont.) |

| Step 3 | Step 3 (cont.) |

Multiple 2 sts + 2.

Special stitch
Tdc2tog (Tunisian double crochet 2 together): Yo, insert hook under next 2 front vertical bars at same time, yo and pull through, yo and pull through 2 loops.

Steps 1–2 Using A for step 1 and B for step 2, work foundation row (see page 16).

Step 3 Using B, ch 1, skip 1st vertical bar, *Tdc2tog, 1 Tdc in next sp (insert hook as for Tfs); rep from * to end, 1 Tdc in end st.

Step 4 Using A, rep step 2.

Step 5 Using A, rep step 3.

Step 6 Rep steps 2–5, changing color as set and ending with step 2.

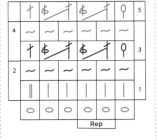

Multiple 2 sts + 2.

Special stitches
Tdc2tog (Tunisian double crochet 2 together): Yo, insert hook under next 2 front vertical bars at same time, yo and pull through, yo and pull through 2 loops.

ETss (extended Tunisian simple stitch): Insert hook from right to left under front vertical bar of st, yo and pull through, ch 1.

Steps 1–2 Work foundation row (see page 16).

Step 3 Ch 1, skip 1st vertical bar, *Tdc2tog, 1 ETss in next sp (insert hook as for Tfs); rep from * to end, 1 Tdc in end st.

Step 4 Rep step 2.

Step 5 Rep steps 3–4.

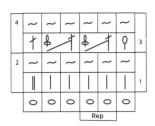

98 Arrows

This stitch produces fabric with good drape and lots of texture while being quite open. It is very easy to work. On one row, you decrease two simple stitches followed by a yarn over. On the next row, you work simple stitches into the decreases and full stitches into the yarn over spaces.

99 Twisted Arrows

Producing a rather dense fabric with little drape but also no curl, this stitch is perfect for a range of homewares and accessories. Treat the yarn over as a stitch and work the twisted knit stitch into the strand created by the yarn over.

Step 3

Step 5

Step 3

Step 5

Multiple 2 sts + 2.

Special stitch
Tss2tog (Tunisian simple stitch 2 together): Insert hook under next 2 front vertical bars at same time, yo and pull through.

Steps 1–2 Work foundation row (see page 16).

Step 3 Skip 1st vertical bar, *Tss2tog, yo; rep from * to end, work end st.

Step 4 Rep step 2.

Step 5 Skip 1st vertical bar, 1 Tss in next st, 1 Tfs in next sp; rep from * to end, work end st.

Step 6 Rep steps 2–5, ending with step 2.

Multiple 2 sts + 2.

Special stitches
Tss2tog: As left.

TwTks (twisted Tunisian knit stitch): Using tip of hook, pull front vertical bar of st (or front strand of yo) to right to reveal back vertical bar, insert hook from front to back through center of st between vertical bars, yo and pull through.

Steps 1–2 Work foundation row (see page 16).

Step 3 Skip 1st vertical bar, *Tss2tog, yo; rep from * to end, work end st.

Step 4 Rep step 2.

Step 5 Skip 1st vertical bar, 1 TwTks in each st to end, work end st.

Step 6 Rep steps 2–5, ending with step 2.

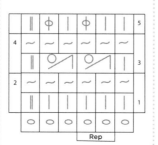

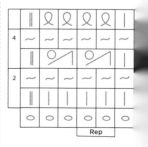

100 Simple Wrap

Alternating rows of color showcase the texture of this stitch. The fabric tends to lean to one side, but good blocking will fix this. Change color by working the first chain of the return pass with the new color. Carry the unused yarn up the side of the work and use it when needed.

101 Mini Wrap

Rows of alternating wraps result in fabric with good drape and lots of visual interest, ideal for a large range of projects from blankets to accessories. To make the wraps, use a cable needle or smaller hook to lift the yarn over and place it over the two stitches just worked.

Step 3

Step 5

Step 3

Step 5

Multiple Any number of sts.

Steps 1–2 Using A for step 1 and B for step 2, work foundation row (see page 16).

Step 3 Using B, skip 1st vertical bar, *yo, 1 Tss in next st, lift yo loop over last st and off hook; rep from * to end, work end st.

Step 4 Using A, rep step 2.

Step 5 Using A, rep step 3.

Step 6 Rep steps 2–5, changing color as set and ending with step 2.

Multiple 2 sts + 2.

Steps 1–2 Work foundation row (see page 16).

Step 3 Skip 1st vertical bar, *yo, 1 Tss in next 2 sts, lift yo loop over last 2 sts and off hook; rep from * to end, work end st.

Step 4 Rep step 2.

Step 5 Skip 1st vertical bar, 1 Tss in next st, *yo, 1 Tss in next 2 sts, lift yo loop over last 2 sts and off hook; rep from * to last st, 1 Tss in next st, work end st.

Step 6 Rep steps 2–5, ending with step 2.

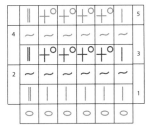

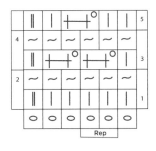

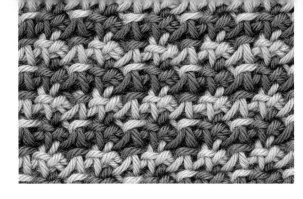

102 Wrapped

This striking stitch has beautiful drape and lends itself perfectly to lots of lacy projects. To create the wrapped stitches, bring the yarn to the front of the work, decrease two simple stitches together, move the yarn to the back of work, and then make a yarn over to replace the decreased stitch. On subsequent rows, treat the yarn over as a stitch by working one stitch of the decrease into the thread of the yarn over. Change color on the return pass when two loops are left on the hook; finish off the pass with the new color. Carry the unused yarn up the side of the work and use it when needed.

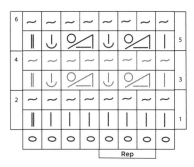

Multiple 3 sts + 2.

Special stitches Tss2tog (Tunisian simple stitch 2 together): Insert hook under next 2 front vertical bars at same time, yo and pull through.

Trs (Tunisian reverse stitch): With yarn and hook at back, insert hook from right to left under back vertical bar of st, yo and pull through.

Steps 1–2 Using A, work foundation row (see page 16).

Step 3 Using B, skip 1st vertical bar, *bring yarn to front, Tss2tog, take yarn to back, yo, 1 Trs in next st; rep from * to end, work end st.

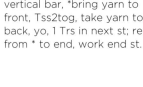

Step 4 Using B, rep step 2.

Step 5 Using A, rep step 3.

Step 6 Using A, rep step 4.

Step 7 Rep steps 3–6, changing color as set.

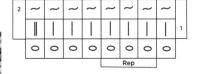

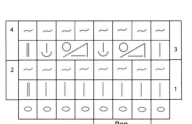

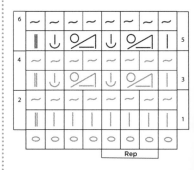

103 Spikes

The spikes are created by working two simple stitches together followed by a yarn under. When working a yarn under, it is paramount that you keep the yarn in place with your index finger the entire time. If the yarn slips, you will create a purl stitch rather than a yarn under. The spike rows are alternated with rows of simple stitch. Change color by working the first chain of the return pass with the new color. Carry the unused yarn up the side of the work and use it when needed.

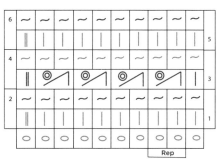

Step 3

Step 5

Multiple 2 sts + 2.

Special stitches Tss2tog (Tunisian simple stitch 2 together): Insert hook under next 2 front vertical bars at same time, yo and pull through.

Yu (yarn under): Bring yarn under hook to front, then wrap it over hook to back (opposite direction from a yarn over); hold wrapped yarn in place on hook with index finger so it does not slip until next st is completed.

Steps 1–2 Using A for step 1 and B for step 2, work foundation row (see page 16).

Step 3 Using B, skip 1st vertical bar, *Tss2tog, yu; rep from * to end, work end st.

Step 4 Using A, rep step 2.

Step 5 Using A, skip 1st vertical bar, 1 Tss in each st to end, work end st.

Step 6 Using B, rep step 2.

Step 7 Rep steps 3–6, changing color as set.

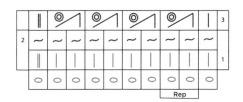

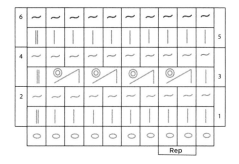

104 Tunisian Lace

Combining yarn overs and Tunisian knit stitch to form a series of square grids, this is a lovely but simple stitch with beautiful drape.

Step 4

Multiple 2 sts + 3.

Steps 1–2 Work foundation row (see page 16).

Step 5

Step 3 Skip 1st vertical bar, yo, skip next st, *1 Tks in next st, yo, skip next st; rep from * to end, work end st.

Step 5 (cont.)

Step 4 Rep step 2.

Step 5 Skip 1st vertical bar, yo, skip next sp, *1 Tks in next st, yo, skip next sp; rep from * to end, work end st.

Step 6 Rep steps 4–5, ending with step 4.

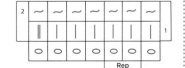

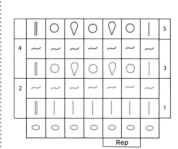

105 Tunisian Mesh

Creating a beautiful mesh with plenty of drape, this stitch is ideal for shawls and wraps. To create a firm edge, work one row of Tunisian simple stitch before binding off.

106 Net

This dense lace stitch is perfect for a variety of different yarns. It can be worked on a smaller hook to achieve a firmer look or on a larger one for more drape.

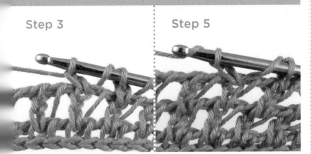

Step 3

Step 5

Multiple 2 sts + 3.

Steps 1–2 Work foundation row (see page 16).

Step 3 Skip 1st vertical bar, ch 2, yo, skip next st, *1 Tks in next st, ch 2, yo, skip next st; rep from * to end, work end st.

Step 4 Rep step 2.

Step 5 Skip 1st vertical bar, ch 2, yo, skip next sp, *1 Tks in next st, ch 2, yo, skip next sp; rep from * to end, work end st.

Step 6 Rep steps 4–5, ending with step 4.

Step 3

Step 5

Multiple 2 sts + 2.

Steps 1–2 Work foundation row (see page 16).

Step 3 Skip 1st vertical bar, *yo, skip next st, 1 Tfs in next sp, skip next st; rep from * to end, work end st.

Step 4 Rep step 2.

Step 5 Skip 1st vertical bar, *1 Tfs in next sp, yo, skip next st; rep from * to end, work end st.

Step 6 Rep step 2.

Step 7 Skip 1st vertical bar, *yo, skip next st, 1 Tfs in next sp; rep from * to end, work end st.

Step 8 Rep steps 4–7, ending with step 4.

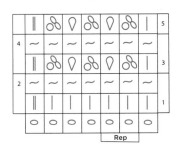

107 Eyelets

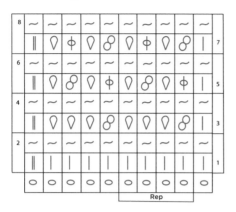

Robust yet airy, this stitch is worked with a combination of double yarn overs and Tunisian full and knit stitches. With excellent drape, the fabric is ideal for lightweight projects. Work through each yarn over individually on the return pass, but treat them as one stitch on the next forward pass.

Step 5

Multiple 4 sts + 2.

Steps 1–2 Work foundation row (see page 16).

Step 3 Skip 1st vertical bar, *[yo] twice, skip next st, 1 Tks in next 3 sts; rep from * to end, work end st.

Step 4 Rep step 2.

Step 5 Skip 1st vertical bar, *1 Tfs in next sp, 1 Tks in next st, [yo] twice, skip next st, 1 Tks in next st; rep from * to end, work end st.

Step 8

Step 6 Rep step 2.

Step 7 Skip 1st vertical bar, *[yo] twice, skip next st, 1 Tks in next st, 1 Tfs in next sp, 1 Tks in next st; rep from * to end, work end st.

Step 8 Rep step 2.

Step 9 Rep steps 5–8.

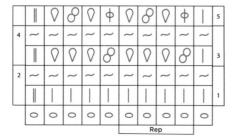

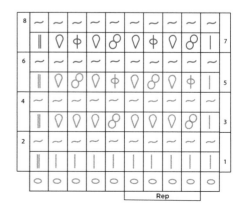

108 Crossed Eyelets

Yarn overs placed between crossed stitches gives this fabric stability and visual interest. Experiment with different yarn weights to achieve interesting textures.

Special stitch Crossed Tks (crossed Tunisian knit stitch): Skip next st, 1 Tks in next st, 1 Tks in skipped st.

109 Crossed Lace

Crossed stitches with chains worked on the return pass produce a fabric with good stability that can be used for a variety of projects.

Special stitch Crossed Tdc (crossed Tunisian double crochet): Skip next 2 sts, 1 Tdc in next st, 1 Tdc in first skipped st (leave center st unworked).

Step 5

Step 7

Step 3

Step 6

Multiple 3 sts + 2.

Steps 1–2 Work foundation row (see page 16).

Step 3 Skip 1st vertical bar, *Crossed Tks, yo, skip next st; rep from * to end, work end st.

Steps 4, 6, 8 Rep step 2.

Step 5 Skip 1st vertical bar, *1 Tks in next 2 sts, yo, skip next sp; rep from * to end, work end st.

Step 7 Skip 1st vertical bar, *Crossed Tks, yo, skip next sp; rep from * to end, work end st.

Step 9 Rep steps 5–8.

Multiple 3 sts + 2.

Steps 1–2 Work foundation row (see page 16).

Step 3 Skip 1st vertical bar, *Crossed Tdc; rep from * to end, work end st.

Step 4 Yo and pull through 1 loop on hook, yo and pull through 2 loops, *ch 1, [yo and pull through 2 loops] twice; rep from * until 1 loop left on hook.

Step 5 Skip 1st vertical bar, 1 Tss in each st and 1 Tfs in each ch-sp to end, work end st.

Step 6 Rep step 2.

Step 7 Rep steps 4–6.

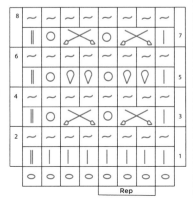

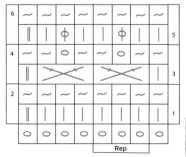

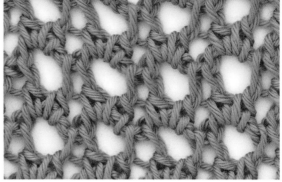

110 Double Lace

This is an excellent stitch for accessories. As with all lace stitches, it will open up beautifully when blocked.

Special stitch Tdc2tog (Tunisian double crochet 2 together): Yo, insert hook under next 2 front vertical bars at same time, yo and pull through, yo and pull through 2 loops.

111 Skipped Lace

This pretty and versatile stitch is created by working two Tunisian double crochets into one space and making two chains on the return pass. The stitch works in a range of yarns, but especially mohair, creating a beautiful and gentle effect.

Step 3

Step 5

Step 4

Step 5

Multiple 3 sts + 2.

Steps 1–2 Work foundation row (see page 16).

Step 3 Skip 1st vertical bar, *Tdc2tog, 1 Tss in next st; rep from * to end, work end st.

Step 4 Yo and pull through 1 loop on hook, yo and pull through 2 loops, *ch 1, [yo and pull through 2 loops] twice; rep from * until 1 loop left on hook.

Step 5 Skip 1st vertical bar, *1 Tss in next st, yo, skip next ch-sp, 1 Tss in next st; rep from * to end, work end st.

Step 6 Rep step 2.

Step 7 Rep steps 3–6.

Multiple 3 sts + 2.

Steps 1–2 Work foundation row (see page 16).

Step 3 Ch 1, skip 1st vertical bar, *skip next st, 2 Tdc in next st, skip next st; rep from * to end, 1 Tdc in end st.

Step 4 Yo and pull through 1 loop on hook, yo and pull through 2 loops, *ch 2, [yo and pull through 2 loops] twice; rep from * until 1 loop left on hook.

Step 5 Ch 1, skip 1st vertical bar, *skip next st, 2 Tdc in next ch-sp (worked as for Tfs), skip next st; rep from * to end, 1 Tdc in end st.

Step 6 Rep step 4.

Step 7 Rep steps 5–6.

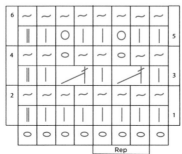

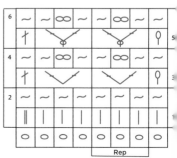

112 Lace Column

The lacy columns are set between columns of Tunisian knit stitch, resulting in a tight fabric that is perfect for projects that require little drape.

Step 3

Step 5

Step 5 (cont.)

Multiple 5 sts + 5.

Steps 1–2 Work foundation row (see page 16).

Step 3 Skip 1st vertical bar, 1 Tks in next 3 sts, *yo, skip next st, 1 Tss in next st, 1 Tks in next 3 sts; rep from * to end, work end st.

Step 4 Rep step 2.

Step 5 Skip 1st vertical bar, 1 Tks in next 3 sts, *1 Tfs in next sp, yo, skip next st, 1 Tks in next 3 sts; rep from * to end, work end st.

Step 6 Rep step 2.

Step 7 Skip 1st vertical bar, 1 Tks in next 3 sts, *yo, skip next st, 1 Tfs in next sp, 1 Tks in next 3 sts; rep from * to end, work end st.

Step 8 Rep step 2.

Step 9 Rep steps 5–8.

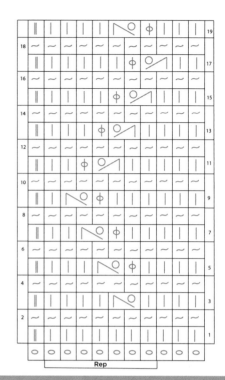

113 Zigzag Lace

This interesting pattern can be used as a single panel or to create several lines of zigzags to add interest to any garment or accessory.

Special stitch Tss2tog (Tunisian simple stitch 2 together): Insert hook under next 2 front vertical bars at same time, yo and pull through.

Rep

| Step 7 | Step 7 (cont.) | Step 11 |

Multiple 7 sts + 4.

Steps 1–2 Work foundation row (see page 16).

Step 3 Skip 1st vertical bar, 1 Tss in next 3 sts, *yo, Tss2tog, 1 Tss in next 5 sts; rep from * to end, ending last rep with 1 Tss in next 4 sts, work end st.

Steps 4, 6, 8, 10, 12, 14, 16, 18 Rep step 2.

Step 5 Skip 1st vertical bar, 1 Tss in next 3 sts, *1 Tfs in next sp, yo, Tss2tog, 1 Tss in next 4 sts; rep from * to end, ending last rep with 1 Tss in next 3 sts, work end st.

Step 7 Skip 1st vertical bar, 1 Tss in next 4 sts, *1 Tfs in next sp, yo, Tss2tog, 1 Tss in

next 4 sts; rep from * to end, ending last rep with 1 Tss in next 2 sts, work end st.

Step 9 Skip 1st vertical bar, 1 Tss in next 5 sts, *1 Tfs in next sp, yo, Tss2tog, 1 Tss in next 4 sts; rep from * to end, ending last rep with 1 Tss in next st, work end st.

Step 11 Skip 1st vertical bar, 1 Tss in next 4 sts, *Tss2tog, yo, 1 Tfs in next sp, 1 Tss in next 4 sts; rep from * to end, ending last rep with 1 Tss in next 2 sts, work end st.

Step 13 Skip 1st vertical bar, 1 Tss in next 3 sts, *Tss2tog, yo, 1 Tfs in next sp, 1 Tss in next 4 sts; rep from * to end, ending last rep with 1 Tss in next 3 sts, work end st.

Step 15 Skip 1st vertical bar, 1 Tss in next 2 sts, *Tss2tog, yo, 1 Tfs in next sp, 1 Tss in next 4 sts; rep from * to end, work end st.

Step 17 Skip 1st vertical bar, 1 Tss in next st, *Tss2tog, yo, 1 Tfs in next sp, 1 Tss in next 4 sts; rep from * to last st, 1 Tss in next st, work end st.

Step 19 Skip 1st vertical bar, 1 Tss in next 2 sts, *1 Tfs in next sp, yo, Tss2tog, 1 Tss in next 4 sts; rep from * to end, work end st.

Step 20 Rep steps 4–19, ending with step 4.

114 Triangle

This sweet triangular lace block can be used as a single motif to add interest to a project, or in rows as a panel for heavier projects such as blankets and pillows.

Special stitch Tss2tog (Tunisian simple stitch 2 together): Insert hook under next 2 front vertical bars at same time, yo and pull through.

Step 5

Step 5 (cont.)

Step 7

Multiple 15 sts + 2.

Steps 1–2 Work foundation row (see page 16).

Step 3 Skip 1st vertical bar, *[yo, Tss2tog, 1 Tss in next st] 4 times, 1 Tss in next 3 sts; rep from * to end, work end st.

Steps 4, 6, 8, 10, 12, 14 Rep step 2.

Step 5 Skip 1st vertical bar, *[1 Tfs in next sp, yo, Tss2tog] 3 times, 1 Tfs in next sp, 1 Tss in next 5 sts; rep from * to end, work end st.

Step 7 Skip 1st vertical bar, *1 Tss in next st, [1 Tfs in next sp, yo, Tss2tog] twice, 1 Tfs in next sp, 1 Tss in next 7 sts; rep from * to end, work end st.

Step 9 Skip 1st vertical bar, *1 Tss in next 2 sts, 1 Tfs in next sp, yo, Tss2tog, 1 Tfs in next sp, 1 Tss in next 9 sts; rep from * to end, work end st.

Step 11 Skip 1st vertical bar, *1 Tss in next 3 sts, 1 Tfs in next sp, 1 Tss in next 11 sts; rep from * to end, work end st.

Step 13 Skip 1st vertical bar, 1 Tss in each st to end, work end st.

Step 15 Rep steps 3–14.

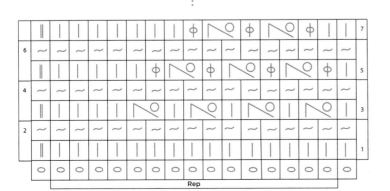

115 Lace Wave

This stunning stitch really comes to life when blocked, opening up all the yarn overs and decreases to showcase the waves. The pattern is surprisingly easy to memorize, even though it has the look of a difficult stitch. It works beautifully in laceweight yarn as a border on a shawl or the edges of garments.

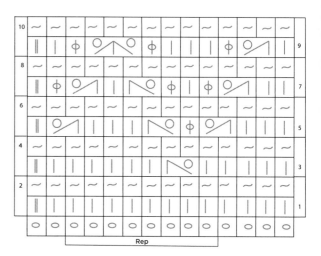

Step 3

Step 5

Step 5 (cont.)

Multiple 8 sts + 6.

Special stitches Tss2tog or Tss3tog (Tunisian simple stitch 2 or 3 together): Insert hook under next 2 or 3 front vertical bars at same time, yo and pull through.

Steps 1–2 Work foundation row (see page 16).

Step 3 Skip 1st vertical bar, 1 Tss in next 4 sts, *yo, Tss2tog, 1 Tss in next 6 sts; rep from * to end, work end st.

Steps 4, 6, 8, 10 Rep step 2.

Step 5 Skip 1st vertical bar, 1 Tss in next 2 sts, *Tss2tog, yo, 1 Tfs in next sp, yo, Tss2tog, 1 Tss in next 3 sts; rep from * to last 2 sts, Tss2tog, yo, work end st.

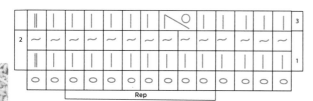

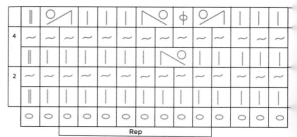

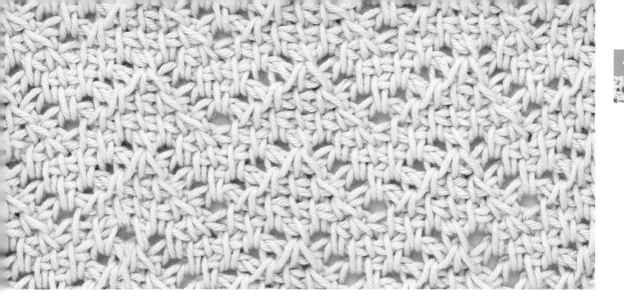

Step 7

Step 7 Skip 1st vertical bar, 1 Tss in next st, *Tss2tog, yo, 1 Tfs in next sp, 1 Tss in next st, 1 Tfs in next sp, yo, Tss2tog, 1 Tss in next st; rep from * to last 3 sts, Tss2tog, yo, 1 Tfs in next sp, work end st.

Step 7 (cont.)

Step 9 Skip 1st vertical bar, Tss2tog, yo, 1 Tfs in next sp, *1 Tss in next 3 sts, 1 Tfs in next sp, yo, Tss3tog, yo, 1 Tfs in next sp; rep from *

Step 9

to last st, 1 Tss in next st, work end st.

Step 11 Rep steps 3–10, from now on working in yo-sps as for Tfs in step 3.

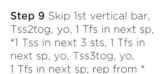

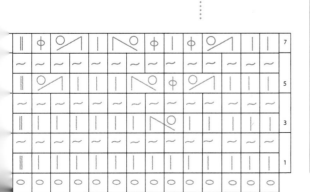

116 Shell Column

Small shells set between columns of Tunisian simple stitch gives this pattern a beautiful and gentle look. The fabric has slight drape and is ideal for firmer projects.

117 Pyramid

Lovely and delicate, this stitch is created by shells worked on the return pass. The stitch has good drape and is perfect for a variety of projects from accessories to homewares.

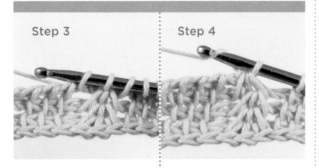

Step 3

Step 4

Step 3

Step 4

Multiple 6 sts + 5.

Step 1 1 Tss in 2nd ch from hook and in each ch to end.

Step 2 Yo and pull through 1 loop on hook, *[yo and pull through 2 loops] 3 times, ch 1, yo and pull through 4 loops (shell made), ch 1; rep from * until 5 loops left on hook,

[yo and pull through 2 loops] 4 times.

Step 3 Skip 1st vertical bar, 1 Tss in next 3 sts, *1 Tfs in next ch-sp, 1 Tss in top of shell, 1 Tfs in next ch-sp, 1 Tss in next 3 sts; rep from * to end, work end st.

Step 4 Rep step 2.

Step 5 Rep steps 3–4.

Multiple 4 sts + 2.

Step 1 1 Tss in 2nd ch from hook and in each ch to end.

Step 2 Yo and pull through 1 loop on hook, yo and pull through 2 loops, *ch 1, yo and pull through 4 loops (shell made), ch 1, yo and pull through 2 loops; rep from * until 1 loop left on hook.

Step 3 Skip 1st vertical bar, *1 Tss in next ch, 1 Tss in top of shell, 1 Tss in next ch, 1 Tks in next st; rep from * to end, work end st.

Step 4 Rep step 2.

Step 5 Rep steps 3–4.

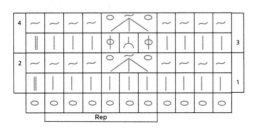

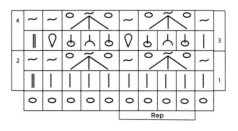

118 Lacy V Stitch

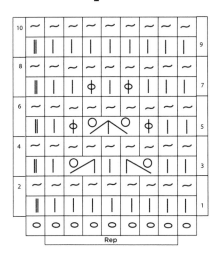

This sweet stitch features a lovely motif that can be used on its own or in a row. The motif is set on a background of Tunisian simple stitch, creating fabric with slight drape. The motifs need to be blocked to open them up.

Step 5

Step 5 (cont.)

Multiple 7 sts + 2.

Special stitches Tss2tog or Tss3tog (Tunisian simple stitch 2 or 3 together): Insert hook under next 2 or 3 front vertical bars at same time, yo and pull through.

Steps 1–2 Work foundation row (see page 16).

Step 3 Skip 1st vertical bar, *1 Tss in next st, yo, Tss2tog, 1 Tss in next st, Tss2tog, yo, 1 Tss in next st; rep from * end, work end st.

Steps 4, 6, 8, 10 Rep step 2.

Step 5 Skip 1st vertical bar, *1 Tss in next st, 1 Tfs in next sp, yo, Tss3tog, yo, 1 Tfs in next sp, 1 Tss in next st; rep from * to end, work end st.

Step 7 Skip 1st vertical bar, *1 Tss in next 2 sts, 1 Tfs in next sp, 1 Tss in next st, 1 Tfs in next sp, 1 Tss in next 2 sts; rep from * to end, work end st.

Step 9 Skip 1st vertical bar, *1 Tss in each st to end, work end st.

Step 11 Rep steps 3–10.

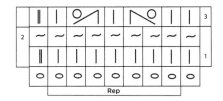

119 Diamond Lace

This stitch creates a beautiful panel of lacy diamonds that is perfect for adding interest to cardigans and sweaters.

Special stitches Tss2tog or Tss3tog (Tunisian simple stitch 2 or 3 together): Insert hook under next 2 or 3 front vertical bars at same time, yo and pull through.

Step 9

Step 15

Multiple 12 sts + 2.

Steps 1–2 Work foundation row (see page 16).

Step 3 Skip 1st vertical bar, *1 Tss in next 3 sts, Tss2tog, yo, 1 Tss in next st, yo, Tss2tog, 1 Tss in next 4 sts; rep from * to end, work end st.

Steps 4, 6, 8, 10, 12, 14, 16, 18, 20 Rep step 2.

Step 5 Skip 1st vertical bar, *1 Tss in next 2 sts, Tss2tog, yo, 1 Tfs in next sp, 1 Tss in next st, 1 Tfs in next sp, yo, Tss2tog, 1 Tss in next 3 sts; rep from * to end, work end st.

Step 7 Skip 1st vertical bar, *1 Tss in next st, Tss2tog, yo, 1 Tfs in next sp, 1 Tss in next 3 sts, 1 Tfs in next sp, yo, Tss2tog, 1 Tss in next 2 sts; rep from * to end, work end st.

Step 9 Skip 1st vertical bar, *Tss2tog, yo, 1 Tfs in next sp, 1 Tss in next 5 sts, 1 Tfs in next sp, yo, Tss2tog, 1 Tss in next st; rep from * to end, work end st.

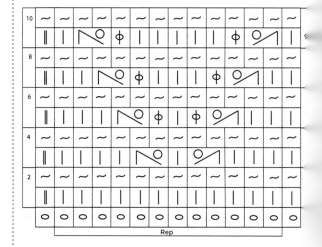

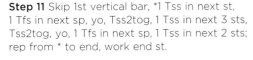

Step 11 Skip 1st vertical bar, *1 Tss in next st, 1 Tfs in next sp, yo, Tss2tog, 1 Tss in next 3 sts, Tss2tog, yo, 1 Tfs in next sp, 1 Tss in next 2 sts; rep from * to end, work end st.

Step 13 Skip 1st vertical bar, *1 Tss in next 2 sts, 1 Tfs in next sp, yo, Tss2tog, 1 Tss in next st, Tss2tog, yo, 1 Tfs in next sp, 1 Tss in next 3 sts; rep from * to end, work end st.

Step 15 Skip 1st vertical bar, *1 Tss in next 3 sts, 1 Tfs in next sp, yo, Tss3tog, yo, 1 Tfs in next sp, 1 Tss in next 4 sts; rep from * to end, work end st.

Step 17 Skip 1st vertical bar, *1 Tss in next 4 sts, 1 Tfs in next sp, yo, skip next st, 1 Tfs in next sp, 1 Tss in next 5 sts; rep from * to end, work end st.

Step 19 Skip 1st vertical bar, *1 Tss in next 3 sts, Tss2tog, yo, 1 Tfs in next sp, yo, Tss2tog, 1 Tss in next 4 sts; rep from * to end, work end st.

Step 21 Rep steps 5–20, ending with step 18.

120 Diamond Spiral

This stunning panel of twisting diamonds is created by a combination of yarn overs and decreases. The diamonds are set on a background of Tunisian simple stitch, perfect for adorning pillows and garments.

Special stitch Tss2tog (Tunisian simple stitch 2 together): Insert hook under next 2 front vertical bars at same time, yo and pull through.

Step 2	Step 9	Step 9 (cont.)
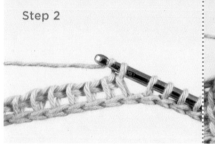		

Multiple 16 sts + 2.

Steps 1–2 Work foundation row (see page 16).

Step 3 Skip 1st vertical bar, *1 Tss in next 5 sts, yo, Tss2tog, 1 Tss in next 2 sts, yo, Tss2tog, 1 Tss in next 5 sts; rep from * to end, work end st.

Steps 4, 6, 8, 10, 12, 14, 16, 18, 20 Rep step 2.

Step 5 Skip 1st vertical bar, *1 Tss in next 3 sts, Tss2tog, yo, 1 Tfs in next sp, yo, Tss2tog, 1 Tss in next st, 1 Tfs in next sp, yo, Tss2tog, 1 Tss in next 4 sts; rep from * to end, work end st.

Step 7 Skip 1st vertical bar, *1 Tss in next 2 sts, Tss2tog, yo, 1 Tfs in next sp, [1 Tss in next st, 1 Tfs in next sp, yo, Tss2tog] twice, 1 Tss in next 3 sts; rep from * to end, work end st.

Step 9 Skip 1st vertical bar, *[1 Tss in next st, Tss2tog, yo, 1 Tfs in next sp] twice, yo, Tss2tog, 1 Tss in next st, 1 Tfs in next sp, yo, Tss2tog, 1 Tss in next 2 sts; rep from * to end, work end st.

Step 11 Skip 1st vertical bar, *[Tss2tog, yo, 1 Tfs in next sp, 1 Tss in next st] twice, [1 Tfs in next sp, yo, Tss2tog, 1 Tss in next st] twice; rep from * to end, work end st.

Step 13 Skip 1st vertical bar, *[1 Tss in next st, 1 Tfs in next sp, yo, Tss2tog] twice, 1 Tss in next st, 1 Tfs in next sp, 1 Tss in next st, Tss2tog, yo, 1 Tfs in next sp, 1 Tss in next 2 sts; rep from * to end, work end st.

Step 15 Skip 1st vertical bar, *1 Tss in next 2 sts, [1 Tfs in next sp, yo, Tss2tog, 1 Tss in next st] twice, Tss2tog, yo, 1 Tfs in next sp, 1 Tss in next 3 sts; rep from * to end, work end st.

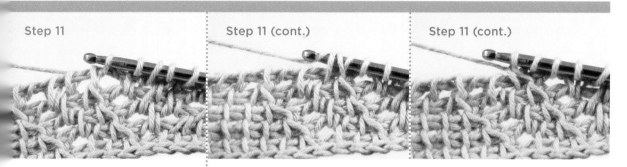

Step 11 **Step 11 (cont.)** **Step 11 (cont.)**

Step 17 Skip 1st vertical bar, *1 Tss in next 3 sts, [1 Tfs in next sp, yo, Tss2tog, 1 Tss in next st] twice, 1 Tfs in next sp, 1 Tss in next 4 sts; rep from * to end, work end st.

Step 19 Skip 1st vertical bar, *1 Tss in next 4 sts, 1 Tfs in next sp, yo, Tss2tog, 1 Tss in next st, 1 Tfs in next sp, yo, Tss2tog, 1 Tss in next 5 sts; rep from * to end, work end st.

Step 21 Rep steps 5–20.

121 Horseshoe

Although this stunning stitch looks complicated, it is in fact simple to work using double yarn overs and decreases. Work through each yarn over individually on the return pass, but treat them as one stitch on the next forward pass.

No stitch—this reflects the arrangement of increases and decreases in the pattern.

Step 3

Step 7

Step 7 (cont.)

Multiple 9 sts + 2.

Special stitch Tss3tog (Tunisian simple stitch 3 together): Insert hook under next 3 front vertical bars at same time, yo and pull through.

Steps 1–2 Work foundation row (see page 16).

Step 3 Skip 1st vertical bar, *[yo] twice, 1 Tss in next 3 sts, Tss3tog, 1 Tss in next 3 sts, [yo] twice; rep from * to end, work end st.

Steps 4, 6, 8, 10, 12 Rep step 2.

Step 5 Skip 1st vertical bar, *1 Tfs in next sp, [yo] twice, 1 Tss in next 2 sts, Tss3tog, 1 Tss in next 2 sts, [yo] twice, 1 Tfs in next sp; rep from * to end, work end st.

Step 7 Skip 1st vertical bar, *1 Tss in next st, 1 Tfs in next sp, [yo] twice, 1 Tss in next st, Tss3tog, 1 Tss in next st, [yo] twice, 1 Tfs in next sp, 1 Tss in next st; rep from * to end, work end st.

Step 9 Skip 1st vertical bar, *1 Tss in next 2 sts, 1 Tfs in

next sp, [yo] twice, Tss3tog, [yo] twice, 1 Tfs in next sp, 1 Tss in next 2 sts; rep from * to end, work end st.

Step 11 Skip 1st vertical bar, 1 Tss in each st and 1 Tfs in each sp to end, work end st.

Step 13 Rep steps 3–12.

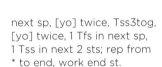

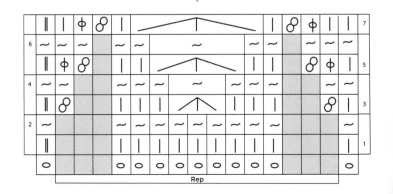

122 Circle

Perfect on its own or in a group, blocking is essential to open up the lace circles. See left for how to treat the double yarn overs.

Special stitches Tss2tog or Tss3tog (Tunisian simple stitch 2 or 3 together): Insert hook under next 2 or 3 front vertical bars at same time, yo and pull through.

Step 7

Step 11

Step 11 (cont.)

Multiple 11 sts + 4.

Steps 1–2 Work foundation row (see page 16).

Step 3 Skip 1st vertical bar, 1 Tss in each st to end, work end st.

Steps 4, 6, 8, 10, 12, 14 Rep step 2.

Step 5 Rep step 3.

Step 7 Skip 1st vertical bar, 1 Tss in next 3 sts, *Tss2tog, [yo] twice, 1 Tss in next st, [yo] twice, Tss2tog, 1 Tss in next 6 sts; rep from * to end, ending last rep with 1 Tss in next 5 sts, work end st.

Step 9 Skip 1st vertical bar, 1 Tss in next 2 sts, *Tss2tog, [yo] twice, 1 Tfs in next sp, 1 Tss in next st, 1 Tfs in next sp, [yo] twice, Tss2tog, 1 Tss in next 4 sts; rep from * to end, work end st.

Step 11 Skip 1st vertical bar, 1 Tss in next 3 sts, *1 Tfs in next sp, [yo] twice, Tss3tog,

[yo] twice, 1 Tfs in next sp, 1 Tss in next 6 sts; rep from * to end, ending last rep with 1 Tss in next 5 sts, work end st.

Step 13 Skip 1st vertical bar, 1 Tss in each st and 1 Tfs in each sp to end, work end st.

Step 15 Rep steps 3–14.

123 Spiral

Gorgeous spiraling leaves make the perfect panel for accessories such as gloves and scarves. The lace eyelets are made using double yarn overs. Work through each yarn over individually on the return pass, but treat them as one stitch on the next forward pass.

No stitch—this reflects the arrangement of increases and decreases in the pattern.

Step 3

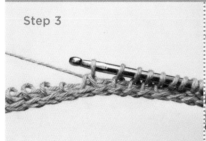

Step 5

Step 5 (cont.)

Multiple 14 sts + 2.

Special stitch Tss2tog (Tunisian simple stitch 2 together): Insert hook under next 2 front vertical bars at same time, yo and pull through.

Steps 1–2 Work foundation row (see page 16).

Step 3 Skip 1st vertical bar, *1 Tps in next 2 sts, [yo] twice, 1 Tss in next 4 sts, Tss2tog, 1 Tss in next 4 sts, 1 Tps in next 2 sts; rep from * to end, work end st.

Steps 4, 6, 8, 10, 12, 14 Rep step 2.

Step 5 Skip 1st vertical bar, *1 Tps in next 2 sts, 1 Tfs in next sp, [yo] twice, 1 Tss in next 4 sts, Tss2tog, 1 Tss in next 3 sts, 1 Tps in next 2 sts; rep from * to end, work end st.

Step 7 Skip 1st vertical bar, *1 Tps in next 2 sts, 1 Tss in next st, 1 Tfs in next sp, [yo] twice, 1 Tss in next 4 sts, Tss2tog, 1 Tss in next 2 sts, 1 Tps in next 2 sts; rep from * to end, work end st.

Step 9 Skip 1st vertical bar, *1 Tps in next 2 sts, 1 Tss in next 2 sts, 1 Tfs in next sp, [yo] twice, 1 Tss in next 4 sts, Tss2tog, 1 Tss in next st, 1 Tps in next 2 sts; rep from * to end, work end st.

Step 11 Skip 1st vertical bar, *1 Tps in next 2 sts, 1 Tss in next 3 sts, 1 Tfs in next sp, [yo] twice, 1 Tss in next 4 sts, Tss2tog, 1 Tps in next 2 sts; rep from * to end, work end st.

Step 13 Skip 1st vertical bar, *1 Tps in next 2 sts, 1 Tss in next 4 sts, 1 Tfs in next sp, 1 Tss in next 5 sts, 1 Tps in next 2 sts; rep from * to end, work end st.

Step 15 Rep steps 3–14.

124 Block Lace

This simple fan pattern looks striking in one or two colors. It is a very pretty stitch and produces a fairly airy fabric with good drape that works well for items that require reversible fabric. The fans are worked on the forward pass.

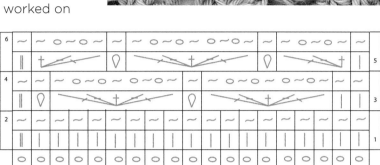

Step 3

Step 3 (cont.)

Step 4

Multiple 8 sts + 3.

Special stitches Fan: Inserting hook as for Tks, work 5 Tdc in same place.

Half Fan: Inserting hook as for Tks, work 3 Tdc in same place.

Steps 1–2 Work foundation row (see page 16).

Step 3 Skip 1st vertical bar, 1 Tss in next st, *skip next 3 sts, Fan in next st, skip next 3 sts, 1 Tks in next st; rep from * to end, work end st.

Step 4 Yo and pull through 1 loop on hook, [yo and pull through 2 loops] twice, *[ch 1, yo and pull through 2 loops] 4 times, [yo and pull through 2 loops] twice; rep from * until 1 loop left on hook.

Step 5 Skip 1st vertical bar, Half Fan in next st, *skip next 2 sts and 2 ch-sps, 1 Tks in next st, skip next 2 ch-sps and 2 sts, Fan in next st; rep from * to end,

ending last rep with Half Fan in next st, work end st.

Step 6 Yo and pull through 1 loop on hook, *[yo and pull through 2 loops, ch 1] twice, [yo and pull through 2 loops] twice, [yo and pull through 2 loops, ch 1] twice; rep from * until 3 loops left on hook, [yo and pull through 2 loops] twice.

Step 7 Rep steps 3–6.

125 Bluebell

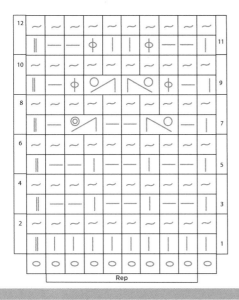

This fairly firm stitch produces fabric with little drape, perfect for homewares. Blocking is essential or the eyelets can become lost in the background stitches.

Step 7

Step 12

Multiple 8 sts + 2.

Special stitches Tss2tog (Tunisian simple stitch 2 together): Insert hook under next 2 front vertical bars at same time, yo and pull through.

Yu (yarn under): Bring yarn under hook to front and then wrap it over hook to back (opposite direction from a yarn over).

Steps 1–2 Work foundation row (see page 16).

Step 3 Skip 1st vertical bar, *1 Tps in next 2 sts, [1 Tss in next st, 1 Tps in next 2 sts] twice; rep from * to end, work end st.

Steps 4, 6, 8, 10, 12 Rep step 2.

Step 5 Rep step 3.

Step 7 Skip 1st vertical bar, *1 Tps in next st, yo, Tss2tog, 1 Tps in next 2 sts, Tss2tog, yu, 1 Tps in next st; rep from * to end, work end st.

Step 9 Skip 1st vertical bar, *1 Tps in next st, 1 Tfs in next sp, yo, [Tss2tog] twice, yo, 1 Tfs in next sp, 1 Tps in next st; rep from * to end, work end st.

Step 11 Skip 1st vertical bar, *1 Tps in next 2 sts, 1 Tfs in next sp, 1 Tss in next 2 sts, 1 Tfs in next sp, 1 Tps in next 2 sts; rep from * to end, work end st.

Step 13 Rep steps 3–12.

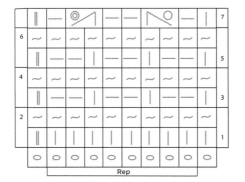

126 Fountain

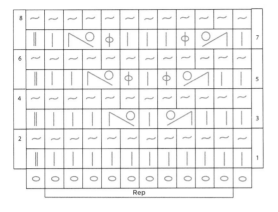

Simple yarn overs and decreases can create the most beautiful lace effects. As with all lace stitches, blocking is essential to open up the stitches and showcase the beauty of the pattern.

Step 3

Step 4

Step 5

Multiple 10 sts + 2.

Special stitch Tss2tog (Tunisian simple stitch 2 together): Insert hook under next 2 front vertical bars at same time, yo and pull through.

Steps 1–2 Work foundation row (see page 16).

Step 3 Skip 1st vertical bar, *1 Tss in next 2 sts, Tss2tog, yo, 1 Tss in next st, yo, Tss2tog, 1 Tss in next 3 sts; rep from * to end, work end st.

Step 4 Rep step 2.

Step 5 Skip 1st vertical bar, *1 Tss in next st, Tss2tog, yo, 1 Tfs in next sp, 1 Tss in next st, 1 Tfs in next sp, yo, Tss2tog, 1 Tss in next 2 sts; rep from * to end, work end st.

Step 6 Rep step 2.

Step 7 Skip 1st vertical bar, *Tss2tog, yo, 1 Tfs in next sp, 1 Tss in next 3 sts, 1 Tfs in next sp, yo, Tss2tog, 1 Tss in next st; rep from * to end, work end st.

Step 8 Rep step 2.

Step 9 Rep steps 3–8.

127 Seed Lace

This stitch produces fabric with an all-over pattern of lacy diamonds alternating from beginning to end of rows. The lace eyelets are made using double yarn overs. Work through each yarn over individually on the return pass, but treat them as one stitch on the next forward pass.

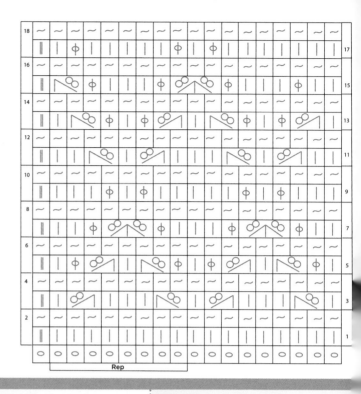

Step 4

Multiple 8 sts + 2.

Special stitches Tss2tog or Tss3tog (Tunisian simple stitch 2 or 3 together): Insert hook under next 2 or 3 front vertical bars at same time, yo and pull through.

Steps 1–2 Work foundation row (see page 16).

Step 3 Skip 1st vertical bar, *[yo] twice, Tss2tog, 1 Tss in next 3 sts, Tss2tog, [yo] twice, 1 Tss in next st; rep from * to end, work end st.

Steps 4, 6, 8, 10, 12, 14, 16, 18 Rep step 2.

Step 5

Step 5 Skip 1st vertical bar, *1 Tfs in next sp, [yo] twice, Tss2tog, 1 Tss in next st, Tss2tog, [yo] twice, 1 Tfs in next sp, 1 Tss in next st; rep from * to end, work end st.

Step 7

Step 7 Skip 1st vertical bar, *1 Tss in next st, 1 Tfs in next sp, [yo] twice, Tss3tog, [yo] twice, 1 Tfs in next sp, 1 Tss in next 2 sts; rep from * to end, work end st.

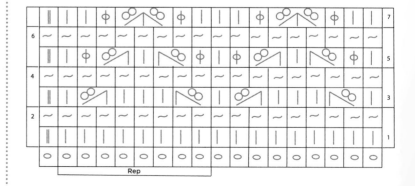

Step 7 (cont.)

Step 9

Step 11

Step 9 Skip 1st vertical bar, *1 Tss in next 2 sts, 1 Tfs in next sp, 1 Tss in next st, 1 Tfs in next sp, 1 Tss in next 3 sts; rep from * to end, work end st.

Step 11 Skip 1st vertical bar, *1 Tss in next st, Tss2tog, [yo] twice, 1 Tss in next st, [yo] twice, Tss2tog, 1 Tss in next 2 sts; rep from * to end, work end st.

Step 13 Skip 1st vertical bar, *Tss2tog, [yo] twice, 1 Tfs in next sp, 1 Tss in next st, 1 Tfs in next sp, [yo] twice, Tss2tog, 1 Tss in next st; rep from * to end, work end st.

Step 15 Skip 1st vertical bar, 1 Tss in next st, *1 Tfs in next sp, 1 Tss in next 3 sts, 1 Tfs in

next sp, [yo] twice, Tss3tog, [yo] twice; rep from * to end, ending last rep with [yo] twice, Tss2tog, work end st.

Step 17 Skip 1st vertical bar, *1 Tss in each st and 1 Tfs in each sp to end, work end st.

Step 19 Rep steps 3–18.

128 Arrowhead Lace

This beautiful panel of lace arrows is set on a background of Tunisian simple stitch with cables framing the lace. This stitch will look beautiful on pillows, blankets, and garments. The lace eyelets are made using double yarn overs. Work through each yarn over individually on the return pass, but treat them as one stitch on the next forward pass.

Step 3

Step 3 (cont.)

Step 5

Multiple 27 sts + 2.

Special stitches Tss2tog (Tunisian simple stitch 2 together): Insert hook under next 2 front vertical bars at same time, yo and pull through.

C4B (cable 4 back): Slip front vertical bars of next 2 sts onto cable needle and hold at back of work, 1 Tss in next 2 sts, 1 Tss in each st on cable needle.

C4F (cable 4 front): Slip front vertical bars of next 2 sts onto cable needle and hold at front of work, 1 Tss in next 2 sts, 1 Tss in each st on cable needle.

Steps 1–2 Work foundation row (see page 16).

Step 3 Skip 1st vertical bar, *1 Tss in next 6 sts, [yo] twice, Tss2tog, 1 Tss in next st, [yo] twice, Tss2tog, 1 Tss in next 5 sts, Tss2tog, [yo] twice, 1 Tss in next st, Tss2tog, [yo] twice,

1 Tss in next 6 sts; rep from * to end, work end st.

Steps 4, 6, 8, 10, 12, 14 Rep step 2.

Step 5 Skip 1st vertical bar, *1 Tss in next st, C4B, 1 Tss in next st, [1 Tfs in next sp, (yo) twice, Tss2tog] twice, 1 Tss in next 3 sts, [Tss2tog, (yo) twice, 1 Tfs in next sp] twice, 1 Tss in next st, C4F, 1 Tss in next st; rep from * to end, work end st.

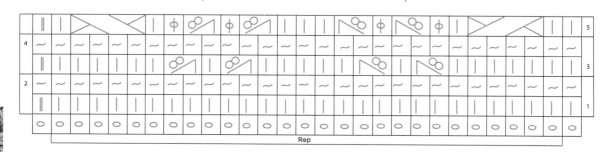

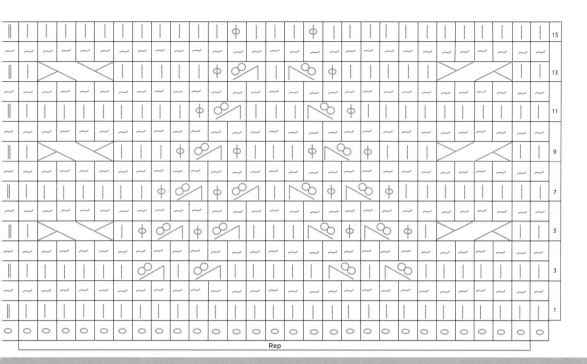

Step 9

Step 9 (cont.)

Step 9 (cont.)

Step 7 Skip 1st vertical bar, *1 Tss in next 7 sts, [1 Tfs in next sp, (yo) twice, Tss2tog] twice, 1 Tss in next st, [Tss2tog, (yo) twice, 1 Tfs in next sp] twice, 1 Tss in next 7 sts; rep from * to end, work end st.

Step 9 Skip 1st vertical bar, *1 Tss in next st, C4B, 1 Tss in next 3 sts, 1 Tfs in next sp, [yo] twice, Tss2tog, 1 Tfs in next sp, 1 Tss in next 3 sts, 1 Tfs in next sp, Tss2tog, [yo] twice, 1 Tfs in next sp, 1 Tss in next 3 sts, C4F, 1 Tss in next st; rep from * to end, work end st.

Step 11 Skip 1st vertical bar, *1 Tss in next 9 sts, 1 Tfs in next sp, [yo] twice, Tss2tog, 1 Tss in next 3 sts, Tss2tog, [yo] twice, 1 Tfs in next sp, 1 Tss in next 9 sts; rep from * to end, work end st.

Step 13 Skip 1st vertical bar, *1 Tss in next st, C4B, 1 Tss in next 5 sts, 1 Tfs in next sp, [yo] twice, Tss2tog, 1 Tss in next st, Tss2tog, [yo] twice, 1 Tfs in next sp, 1 Tss in next 5 sts, C4F, 1 Tss in next st; rep from * to end, work end st.

Step 15 Skip 1st vertical bar, 1 Tss in each st and 1 Tfs in each sp to end, work end st.

Step 16 Rep steps 2–15, ending with step 2.

129 Chevron I

This traditional chevron is a useful stitch that lends itself to a wide variety of projects ranging from accessories to homewares. The interesting pattern is created using Tunisian simple stitch, yarn overs, and decreases. The yarn over spaces are filled with stitches on subsequent rows.

Step 2

Multiple 14 sts + 2.

Special stitch Tss3tog (Tunisian simple stitch 3 together): Insert hook under next 3 front vertical bars at same time, yo and pull through.

Steps 1–2 Work foundation row (see page 16).

Step 3

Step 3 Skip 1st vertical bar, *yo, 1 Tss in next 5 sts, Tss3tog, 1 Tss in next 5 sts, yo, 1 Tss in next st; rep from * to end, work end st.

Step 4 Rep step 2.

Step 3 (cont.)

Step 5 Rep steps 3–4, from now on working in yo-sps as for Tfs in step 3.

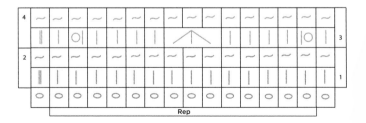

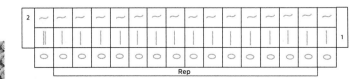

130 Chevron II

This smaller variation of the previous stitch is created by having fewer stitches between the points and troughs of the chevrons. The yarn over spaces are filled with stitches on subsequent rows. Stripes of two colors add interest, but you can work this stitch in as many color combinations as you like. Change color on the return pass when two loops are left on the hook; finish off the pass with the new color. Carry the unused yarn up the side of the work and use it when needed.

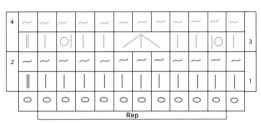

Step 3

Multiple 10 sts + 2.

Special stitch Tss3tog (Tunisian simple stitch 3 together): Insert hook under next 3 front vertical bars at same time, yo and pull through.

Steps 1–2 Using A, work foundation row (see page 16).

Step 3 (cont.)

Step 3 Using B, skip 1st vertical bar, *yo, 1 Tss in next 3 sts, Tss3tog, 1 Tss in next 3 sts, yo, 1 Tss in next st; rep from * to end, work end st.

Step 4 Using B, rep step 2.

Step 5 Rep steps 3–4, from now on working in yo-sps as for Tfs in step 3 and changing color every two rows.

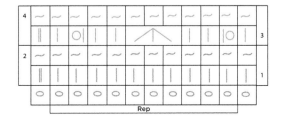

131 Wave Stitch

This is a good introduction to Tunisian wave patterns. A sense of movement is created by working groups of stitches of different heights in the same row. These groups of stitches alternate every two rows and are interrupted by rows of Tunisian simple stitch. The wave pattern looks great in single or multiple colors. Change color on the return pass when two loops are left on the hook; finish off the pass with the new color. Carry the unused yarn up the side of the work and use it when needed.

Step 2

Multiple 10 sts + 3.

Special stitch Ttr (Tunisian treble crochet): [yo] twice, insert hook from right to left under front vertical bar of st, yo and pull through, [yo and pull through 2 loops on hook] twice.

Steps 1–2 Using A, work foundation row (see page 16).

Step 3

Step 3 Using B, skip 1st vertical bar, *1 Tss in next 2 sts, 1 Tdc in next 2 sts, 1 Ttr in next 3 sts, 1 Tdc in next 2 sts, 1 Tss in next st; rep from * to last st, 1 Tss in next st, work end st.

Step 4 Using B, rep step 2.

Step 5

Step 5 Using A, skip 1st vertical bar, 1 Tss in each st to end, work end st.

Step 6 Using A, rep step 2.

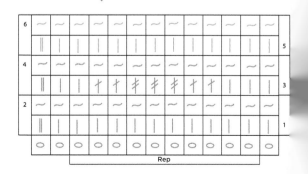

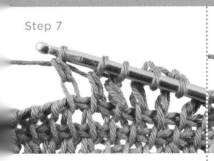

Step 7 Using B, ch 2, skip 1st vertical bar, *1 Ttr in next 2 sts, 1 Tdc in next 2 sts, 1 Tss in next 3 sts, 1 Tdc in next 2 sts, 1 Ttr in next st; rep from * to last st, 1 Ttr in next st, 1 Ttr in end st.

Step 8 Using B, rep step 2.

Steps 9–10 Using A, rep steps 5–6.

Step 11 Rep steps 3–10, changing color as set.

132 Stream

The small, gently flowing waves in this pattern look attractive in one or many colors. The fabric has good drape and can be used to create a full project, or as just a few rows to add interest to the edging of a cardigan. Change color on the return pass when two loops are left on the hook; finish off the pass with the new color. Carry the unused yarn up the side of the work and use it when needed.

Step 5

Step 5 (cont.)

Step 6

Multiple 6 sts + 6.

Steps 1–2 Using A, work foundation row (see page 16).

Step 3 Using B, ch 1, skip 1st vertical bar, 1 Tdc in next 2 sts, *1 Tss in next 3 sts, 1 Tdc in next 3 sts; rep from * to last 2 sts, 1 Tss in next 2 sts, work end st.

Step 4 Using B, rep step 2.

Step 5 Using C, skip 1st vertical bar, 1 Tss in next 2 sts, *1 Tdc in next 3 sts, 1 Tss in next 3 sts; rep from * to last 2 sts, 1 Tdc in next 2 sts, 1 Tdc in end st.

Step 6 Using C, rep step 2.

Step 7 Rep steps 2–6, changing color as set.

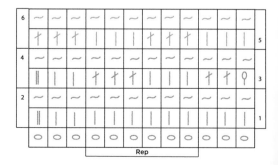

133 Gentle Wave

A beautiful and gentle stitch with a slight wave, this pattern produces fabric with very good drape that is perfect for a large number of projects, from garments to homewares. The yarn over spaces are filled with stitches on subsequent rows.

No stitch—this reflects the arrangement of increases and decreases in the pattern.

Step 3

Multiple 12 sts + 3.

Special stitch Tss2tog (Tunisian simple stitch 2 together): Insert hook under next 2 front vertical bars at same time, yo and pull through.

Steps 1–2 Work foundation row (see page 16).

Step 3 (cont.)

Step 3 Skip 1st vertical bar, 1 Tss in next st, *[Tss2tog] twice, [yo, 1 Tss in next st] 3 times, yo, [Tss2tog] twice, 1 Tss in next st; rep from * to end, work end st.

Step 4 Rep step 2.

Step 5

Step 5 Skip 1st vertical bar, *1 Tss in next 3 sts, [1 Tfs in next sp, 1 Tss in next st] 4 times, 1 Tss in next st; rep from * to last st, 1 Tss in next st, work end st.

Step 6 Rep step 2.

Step 7 Rep steps 3–6.

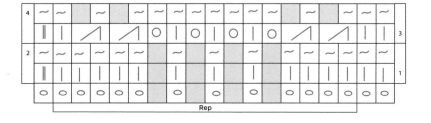

134 Easy Wave

The gentle movement of this easy wave pattern is created by working two rows of waves interrupted by a row of Tunisian purl stitch in a contrast color. Change color on the return pass when two loops are left on the hook; finish off the pass with the new color. Carry the unused yarn up the side of the work and use it when needed.

Step 5

Multiple 6 sts + 6.

Steps 1–2 Using A, work foundation row (see page 16).

Step 3 Using B, skip 1st vertical bar, 1 Tss in next 2 sts, *1 Tdc in next 3 sts, 1 Tss in next 3 sts; rep from * to last 2 sts, 1 Tdc in next 2 sts, 1 Tdc in end st.

Step 4 Using B, rep step 2.

Step 5 (cont.)

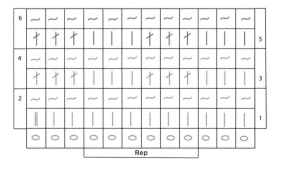

Steps 5–6 Using B, rep steps 3–4.

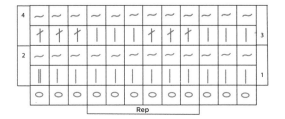

Step 9 Using B, ch 1, skip 1st vertical bar, 1 Tdc in next 2 sts, *1 Tss in next 3 sts, 1 Tdc in next 3 sts; rep from * to last 2 sts, 1 Tss in next 2 sts, work end st.

Step 10 Using B, rep step 2.

Steps 11–12 Using B, rep steps 9–10.

Steps 13–14 Using A, rep steps 7–8.

Step 15 Rep steps 3–14, changing color as set.

Step 7

Step 7 Using A, skip 1st vertical bar, 1 Tps in each st to end, work end st.

Step 8 Using A, rep step 2.

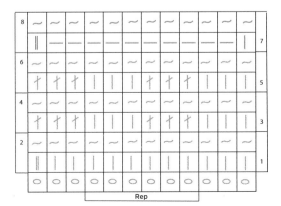

135 Shell Wave

A stunning stitch that is equally beautiful in one or multiple colors, the deep waves are created by working rows of increases and decreases interrupted by rows of Tunisian purl stitch. Treat the yarn overs as a stitch and work into them as for Tps in the usual way on the purl rows.

Step 3	Step 3 (cont.)	Step 5
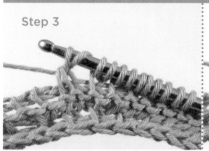		

Multiple 18 sts + 3.

Special stitch Tss2tog (Tunisian simple stitch 2 together): Insert hook under next 2 front vertical bars at same time, yo and pull through.

Steps 1–2 Work foundation row (see page 16).

Step 3 Skip 1st vertical bar, *1 Tss in next st, [Tss2tog] 3 times, [yo, 1 Tss in next st] 5 times, yo, [Tss2tog] 3 times; rep from * to last st, 1 Tss in next st, work end st.

Step 4 Rep step 2.

Step 5 Skip 1st vertical bar, *1 Tps in each st to end, work end st.

Step 6 Rep step 2.

Step 7 Rep steps 3–6.

☐ No stitch—this reflects the arrangement of increases and decreases in the pattern.

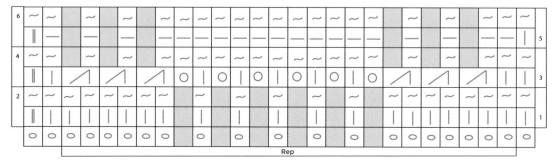

136 Honeycomb Wave

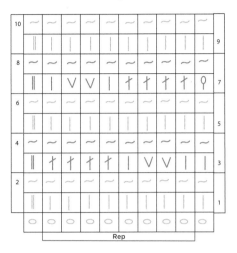

This classic wave stitch creates a striking pattern that lends itself perfectly to blankets and homewares. Change color on the return pass when two loops are left on the hook; finish off the pass with the new color. Carry the unused yarn up the side of the work and use it when needed.

Step 3

Step 5

Step 7

Multiple 8 sts + 2.

Steps 1–2 Using A, work foundation row (see page 16).

Step 3 Using B, skip 1st vertical bar, *1 Tss in next st, 1 Tslst in next 2 sts, 1 Tss in next st, 1 Tdc in next 4 sts; rep from * to end, work end st.

Step 4 Using B, rep step 2.

Step 5 Using A, skip 1st vertical bar, 1 Tss in each st to end, work end st.

Step 6 Using A, rep step 2.

Step 7 Using B, ch 1, skip 1st vertical bar, *1 Tdc in next 4 sts, 1 Tss in next st, 1 Tslst in next 2 sts, 1 Tss in

next st; rep from * to end, work end st.

Step 8 Using B, rep step 2.

Steps 9–10 Using A, rep steps 5–6.

Step 11 Rep steps 3–10, changing color as set.

137 Cross Stitch

Tunisian simple stitch creates the perfect grid for cross stitch. You can use any cross stitch chart to embroider on your work. Use the same or slightly thicker yarn to cross stitch onto your background. You will need a tapestry needle.

Step 2

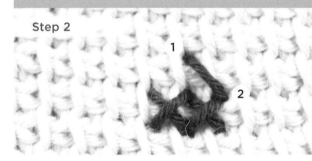

Step 3

Step 1 Thread tapestry needle with chosen color and secure the thread with a small stitch at the back of the work, leaving a tail to weave in at the end of the project.

Step 2 Bring needle through to front of work just above top left corner of horizontal bar of stitch (point 1) and pull yarn through. Take needle over and across to bottom right corner of vertical bar of stitch (point 2) and pull yarn through to back of work.

Step 3 Bring needle up just below bottom left corner of horizontal bar of stitch (point 3) and pull yarn through to front of work. Take needle over and across to top right corner of vertical bar of stitch (point 4) and pull yarn through to back of work to complete one cross stitch.

Step 4 Rep steps 2–3 to work each cross stitch.

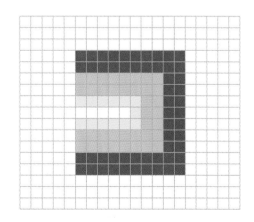

138 Duplicate Stitch

Also known as Swiss darning, this is a great way to embellish your crochet. It only works on Tunisian knit stitch, which creates the perfect *V* shape for duplicate stitch. Use the same or slightly thicker yarn than the one used for the base of the project. You will need a tapestry needle.

139 Surface Slip Stitch

This stitch is perfect for adding interest to plain Tunisian crochet fabric, and works well in straight or curved lines. The stitches are formed by working slip stitches from front to back of the work.

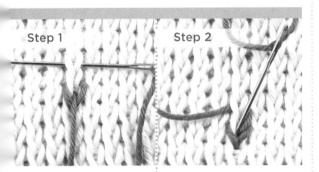

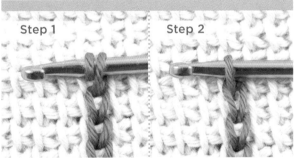

Step 1 Thread tapestry needle and insert from back to front of work at base of stitch (point of *V*). Then insert needle from right to left under two legs of V-shaped stitch above and pull yarn through.

Step 2 Insert needle back into same place as starting point of duplicate stitch (point of *V*) and pull yarn through.

Step 3 Rep steps 1–2 to work each duplicate stitch.

Step 1 Insert hook in desired stitch from front to back of work, yo and pull through to front. Insert hook in next stitch to back of work, yo and pull through (2 loops on hook).

Step 2 Pull 2nd loop through 1st loop on hook.

Step 3 Rep steps 1–2 to work each surface slip stitch.

140 Surface Slip Stitch over Mesh

Working surface slip stitch over Tunisian crochet mesh gives you the opportunity to play with yarns of different textures and weight. This embellishment would look beautiful on a wrap. The Tunisian mesh pattern on page 113 has been used as the base for surface slip stitch here.

Step 1 Join yarn to starting row of work with slip stitch, keeping yarn at back of work.

Step 2 Insert hook from front to back in next st, yo and pull through (2 loops on hook).

Step 3 Pull 2nd loop through 1st loop on hook. Ch 1, insert hook over next row of mesh to back of work, yo and pull through work and loop on hook.

Step 4 Rep steps 2–3 to work each surface slip stitch.

141 Weaving

Weaving is a beautiful way to embellish Tunisian simple stitch. Not only does it create interesting pieces, but it also stiffens and strengthens the fabric. There is no limit with weaving; you can weave in any direction and with any yarn. You will need a tapestry needle.

142 Beaded Stitch

Beads are a beautiful way to add an extra dimension to your work. Beads look stunning on Tunisian simple stitch or added to Tunisian lace.

Step 1   Step 2

Step 1 Thread tapestry needle and pull through to front of work. Insert needle under vertical bars of stitches in whichever direction you choose.

Step 2 Pull yarn through the stitches. When weaving is complete, secure yarn at back.

Step 3 Rep steps 1–2 for each section of weaving in same color.

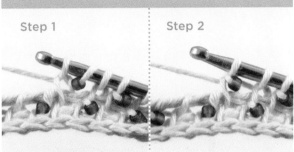

Step 1   Step 2

Preparation Before starting to crochet, thread beads onto yarn. To do this, thread a fine sewing needle (one that will easily pass through the beads) with sewing thread. Knot ends of thread to form a loop, then pass end of yarn through this loop. Thread a bead onto sewing needle and gently slide it onto the yarn. Continue in this way until required numbers of beads are on the yarn.

Step 1 Slide a bead up the yarn close to the work, yo, insert hook in next stitch as for Tss, yo and pull through, slide bead to front of work.

Step 2 Pull loop through yarn over.

Step 3 Rep steps 1–2 to work each beaded stitch.

143 V Stitch Edging

Suitable for many types of projects, this edging works up very quickly. Finish with standard crochet slip stitch, inserting the hook as for Tss.

Special stitches Double V st: Inserting hook as for Tks, work [1 Tdc, yo, 1 Tdc] in same st.

Picot: [1 sl st, ch 3, 1 sl st] in next ch-sp.

144 Wave Edging

This classic wave stitch creates a striking edge that lends itself perfectly to blankets and other homewares. Change color on the return pass when two loops are left on the hook; finish off the pass with the new color. Finish with standard crochet slip stitch, inserting the hook as for Tss.

Step 3

Step 5

Step 5

Step 7

Multiple 3 sts + 2.

Steps 1–2 Work foundation row (see page 16).

Step 3 Skip 1st vertical bar, *skip next st, Double V st in next st, skip next st; rep from * to end, work end st.

Step 4 Yo and pull through 1 loop on hook, [yo and pull

through 2 loops] 3 times, *ch 1, [yo and pull through 2 loops] 3 times; rep from * until 1 loop left on hook.

Step 5 Skip 1st vertical bar, 1 sl st in next 3 sts, *Picot, 1 sl st in next 3 sts; rep from * to end, 1 sl st in end st.

Multiple 8 sts + 2.

Steps 1–2 Using A, work foundation row (see page 16).

Step 3 Using A, skip 1st vertical bar, *1 Tss in next st, 1 Tslst in next 2 sts, 1 Tss in next st, 1 Tdc in next 4 sts; rep from * to end, work end st.

Step 4 Using A, rep step 2.

Step 5 Using B, skip 1st vertical bar, *1 Tdc in next 4 sts, 1 Tss in next st, 1 Tslst in next 2 sts, 1 Tss in next st; rep from * to end, work end st.

Step 6 Using B, rep step 2.

Step 7 Using B, skip 1st vertical bar, 1 Tss in each st to end, work end st.

Step 8 Using B, rep step 2, then work 1 sl st in each st to end.

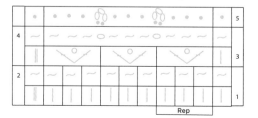

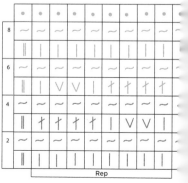

145 Fan Edging

This bold edging works well on delicate projects. It is also useful for household items such as pillows and dishcloths. Finish with standard crochet slip stitch, inserting the hook as for Tss.

146 Picot Edging

Cute and playful, this sweet edging is created by picots worked along the edge with slip stitches. The edging will add charm to any project. Finish with standard crochet slip stitch, inserting the hook as for Tss.

Step 3	Step 4	Step 3	Step 3 (cont.)

Multiple 6 sts + 1.

Special stitch Fan: Inserting hook as for Tks, work 5 Tdc in same st.

Steps 1–2 Work foundation row (see page 16).

Step 3 Skip 1st vertical bar, skip next 2 sts, Fan in next st,

skip next 2 sts, *1 Tslst in next st, skip next 2 sts, Fan in next st, skip next 2 sts; rep from * to end, work end st.

Step 4 Rep step 2, then work 1 sl st in each st to end.

Multiple 3 sts + 2.

Special stitch Picot: Ch 3, 1 sl st in next st.

Steps 1–2 Work foundation row (see page 16).

Step 3 Skip 1st vertical bar, *1 sl st in next st, Picot; rep from * to end, 1 sl st in end st.

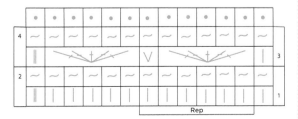

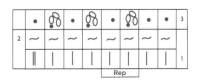

147 Striped Edging

This edging is simple but the change of colors gives it an interesting look. The edging curls and requires steaming when finished. Change color by working the first chain of the return pass with the new color. Finish with standard crochet slip stitch, inserting the hook as for Tss.

148 Puff Edging

This playful edging is perfect for heavier weight projects such as blankets, and would look just as charming in one color. It needs to be steam blocked. Refer to the stitch introduction on page 44 for guidance on changing colors to work the puffs. Finish with standard crochet slip stitch, inserting the hook as for Tss.

Step 7	Step 8

Step 5	Step 5 (cont.)

Multiple 2 sts + 2.

Steps 1–2 Using A for step 1 and B for step 2, work foundation row (see page 16).

Step 3 Using B, skip 1st vertical bar, 1 Tss in each st to end, work end st.

Step 4 Using C, rep step 2.

Step 5 Using C, skip 1st vertical bar, 1 Tss in each st to end, work end st.

Step 6 Using A, rep step 2.

Step 7 Using A, skip 1st vertical bar, *1 Tss in next st, 1 Tps in next st; rep from * to end, work end st.

Step 8 Using B, rep step 2, then work 1 sl st in each st to end.

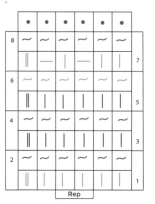

Multiple 4 sts + 5.

Special stitch Puff— hdc5tog (half double crochet 5 together): [yo, insert hook as for Tks, yo and pull loop through] 5 times in same st, yo and pull through 10 loops on hook.

Steps 1–2 Using A, work foundation row (see page 16).

Step 3 Using A, skip 1st vertical bar, 1 Tss in each st to end, work end st.

Step 4 Using A, rep step 2.

Step 5 Using A, skip 1st vertical bar, 1 Tss in next st, using B, Puff in next st, *using A, 1 Tss in next 3 sts, using B, Puff in next st; rep from * to last st, using A, 1 Tss in next st, work end st.

Step 6 Using A, rep step 2, then work 1 sl st in each st to end.

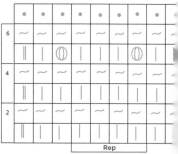

149 Lace Edging

Beautiful and light, this lacy edging is created by yarn overs. It will complement any lightweight project, such as scarves and wraps, but it will also look perfect on blankets.

150 Seed Edging

This great edging is worked sideways and joined to the edge of the project as you go. Seed stitch prevents the edge from curling and gives the project some texture. The edging works on any of number of stitches. Finish with standard crochet slip stitch, inserting the hook as for Tss.

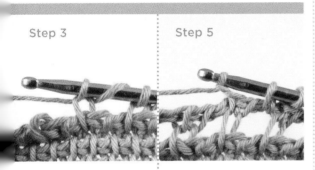

Step 3   Step 5

Step 3   Step 5

Multiple 2 sts + 2.

Steps 1–2 Work foundation row (see page 16).

Step 3 Skip 1st vertical bar, yo, skip next st, *1 Tss in next st, yo, skip next st; rep from * to end, work end st.

Step 4 Rep step 2.

Step 5 Skip 1st vertical bar, 1 Tfs in next sp, *1 Tps in next st, 1 Tfs in next sp; rep from * to end, work end st.

Step 6 Rep step 2.

Multiple 2 sts + 1.

Steps 1–2 Join yarn to 1st st on edge of project with sl st, ch 5 (or required multiple), then work foundation row (see page 16).

Step 3 Skip 1st vertical bar, *1 Tps in next st, 1 Tss in next st; rep from * to end, 1 sl st in next st on edge of project.

Step 4 Rep step 2.

Step 5 Skip 1st vertical bar, *1 Tss in next st, 1 Tps in next st; rep from * to end,

1 sl st in next st on edge of project.

Step 6 Rep step 2.

Step 7 Rep steps 3–6 until each st on edge of project is worked, then work 1 sl st in each st to end.

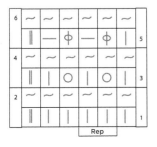

join to project →

2 Tunisian Crochet Skills

From learning about Tunisian hooks to stitch variations and finishing techniques, this chapter walks you through the essentials of Tunisian crocheting. Basic stitches and useful techniques are covered with step-by-step instructions and illustrated with clear line drawings, so you can develop your skills and become a confident Tunisian crocheter.

Yarn

With such an amazing variety of yarns on the market, we are truly spoiled for choice. They come in a kaleidoscope of colors and a wide range of weights, and they are all suitable for Tunisian crochet.

YARN WEIGHT
Yarn weight refers to the thickness of the yarn; the ball band provides this information. It also gives you a recommendation of the size of knitting needles or crochet hook to use with the specific yarn. Tunisian crochet produces denser fabric because of the structure of the stitches, so it is recommended to always go 1 or 2 sizes up in hook size.

Lace/superfine: Very fine yarns used mostly for delicate openwork.

Sport: Fine yarns used for most types of work, producing a lightweight fabric. This weight in wool with nylon is perfect for making socks.

Light worsted/DK (double knitting): The most commonly used weight of yarn producing medium-weight garments, light worsted and DK are suitable for most types of Tunisian crochet, from plain to lace or textured.

Worsted/aran: Both slightly thicker than light worsted, worsted is lighter than aran, but both weights can be used for a large number of projects.

Bulky: Works up fast and is used for a range of projects, including hats, scarves, and garments. It produces a heavy-weight fabric with great stitch definition.

Super bulky: Perfect for supersized cuddly designs, it works up superfast and is perfect for hats, scarves, and cozy garments.

YARN WEIGHTS

Yarn is categorized by the thickness of each strand, known as its weight. This table shows the most common weight categories, with the standard crochet gauge range and hook sizes.

Category	Names	Gauge range to 4in (10cm)	Hook size range
0 Lace	fingering, 2-ply, 10-count crochet thread	32–42 single crochet stitches	steel 6-8 (1.6-1.4mm); regular B (2.25mm)
1 Superfine	sock, fingering, baby	21–32 single crochet stitches	B-E (2.25-3.5mm)
2 Fine	sport, 4-ply, baby	16–20 single crochet stitches	E-7 (3.5-4.5mm)
3 Light	light worsted, DK	12–17 single crochet stitches	7-I (4.5-5.5mm)
4 Medium	worsted, aran, afghan	11–14 single crochet stitches	I-K (5.5-6.5mm)
5 Bulky	bulky, craft, rug	8–11 single crochet stitches	K-M (6.5-9mm)
6 Super bulky	super bulky, roving	7-9 single crochet stitches	M-Q (9-15mm)
7 Jumbo	jumbo, roving	6 or fewer single crochet stitches	Q (15mm) and larger

YARN FIBER

Yarns are made of many natural fibers such as alpaca and wool, or manmade fibers such as acrylic and nylon, all of which come in a range of thicknesses.

1. Wool

This very warm fiber is the most popular for crochet and knitting. It comes from the fleece of sheep, and different breeds have different names of wool. Merino wool is one of those types that comes from merino sheep, as is Shetland and Botany. Wool yarns are easy to crochet with and have wonderful bounce.

2. Cotton

This fiber comes in different grades of softness, with Egyptian cotton being the softest. Cotton is a very kind fiber on the skin and suits a lot of people with skin allergies. Cotton shows off stitch definition beautifully, but it can be heavy and less elastic than wool. However, it does have superb drape.

3. Mixed yarns

There is a vast array of mixed yarns on the market. They are made by plying different fibers together to produce different textures and weights. They can be natural fibers mixed with synthetic, such as wool and nylon, producing great sock yarn, or all natural, such as mohair and silk or wool and cotton.

4. Novelty yarns

These yarns are mostly spun from manmade fibers and are made of several plies twisted together. They are perfect for a variety of plain projects that will showcase the yarn.

5. Manmade fibers

Synthetic fibers are made from crudes and intermediates, including petroleum, coal, limestone, and water. The most common fiber is acrylic, which mimics natural fibers such as wool. Because they are manmade or semi-manmade, they are cheaper and longer, making them more budget-friendly.

6. Bamboo and soya yarns

These are environmentally friendly yarns. Bamboo is made from the center of the bamboo stalk; it is a soft yarn with very good drape. Soya yarns are made from soya plant; they are incredibly soft and can often mimic silk yarns.

Equipment

Very little equipment is necessary for Tunisian crochet.
All you really need is a hook to get started, although items
such as pins and sharp scissors are useful accessories.

HOOKS

Tunisian crochet hooks,
also knows as Afghan
hooks, are similar to
standard crochet hooks
but with one difference:
they are a lot longer as
you need to gather
all the stitches on the
hook on forward passes.
Hooks come in many
different types and sizes.
They are usually made
from steel aluminum
(suitable for most fibers),
plastic, wood, or bamboo
(lightweight and easy
on the hands). Some
crocheters choose a
hook depending on
which fiber they want
to work with, so that
it is easy on the hands.
My personal preference
is a wooden hook.

1. Rigid hook

This is a long hook up to
14in (35cm) in length and
comes with a stopper at
the end. These are the
most commonly available
Tunisian crochet hooks.
They are not suitable
for large projects as the
stitches gathering on
the hook can make them
very heavy to hold.

2. Flexible hook

These have a flexible
cable attached to a
crochet hook. The hook
is usually the length of
a standard crochet hook,
and the cables come
in different lengths.
Some have the cable
permanently fixed to the
hook, while others are
interchangeable, so that
the cable length can be
adjusted to suit the
project or attached to
different-sized hooks.
   Interchangeable hooks
are becoming a lot more
popular among Tunisian
crocheters as they are
very flexible. The hook
comes with a fastening
device at the end for
attaching the cable.
This can be a screw-in
or a clip-in, depending
on the manufacturer.

3. Double-ended hook

These are often used
for working in the round,
and come in lengths
up to 14in (35cm). Do
not confuse these with
standard double-ended
crochet hooks, which
usually have different
sizes on each end and
are not designed for
Tunisian crochet.

4. Standard crochet hook

If you are making a
small project, a standard
smooth hook will do just
fine. Make sure it does
not have a handle (such
as a comfort grip), and
put a stopper at the end
to stop the stitches from
slipping off. A knitting
needle point protector
works great as a stopper.

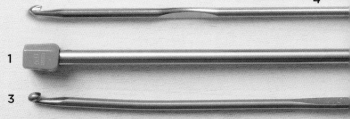

2

4

1

3

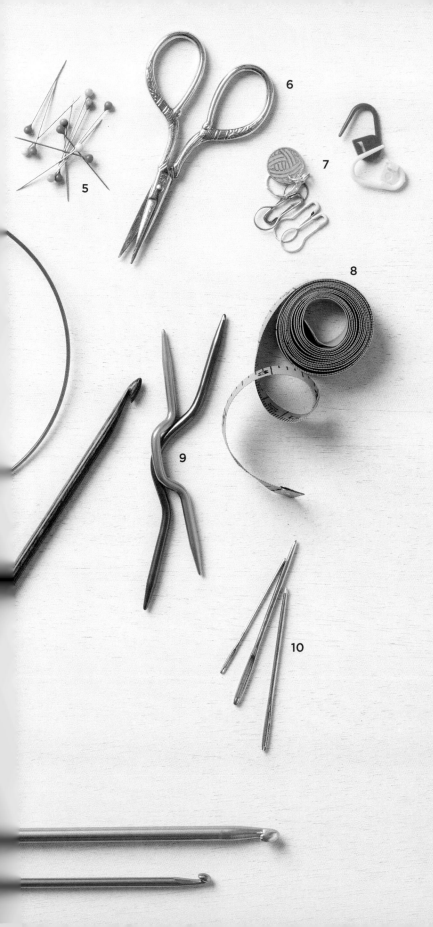

ACCESSORIES

5. Pins
Choose rust-resistant pins with large heads for pinning out your work when blocking.

6. Scissors
Sharp scissors are a must for any crocheter. Small, sharp embroidery scissors are best for snipping yarn.

7. Stitch markers
These can be slipped onto a particular stitch or row and aid in counting. When working in the round, they can be placed to denote the beginning and end of the round.

8. Tape measure
This is essential for checking gauge and the length or width of a project. Retractable tape measures are most useful as they fit neatly into your project bag.

9. Cable needle
Needles for working cable patterns come in different styles and sizes. Cranked cable needles are very useful as the slipped stitches sit neatly in the crank of the needle and do not move. Straight cable needles are a good choice as well, but the stitches can slip off them when working on the cable twist.

10. Tapestry needle
Blunt-ended needles are essential for weaving in ends and sewing up projects. Make sure the eye is large enough to thread the yarn through.

Getting Started

HOLDING THE HOOK

Most people find it more comfortable to hold a Tunisian crochet hook like a knife. This way you will have the most control over the hook, allowing for better grip and more room for the gathering stitches. Also, it will give you better movement on return passes. Grasp the hook between the thumb and index finger of the right hand, as if holding a knife, with the hook facing downward.

MAKING A SLIP KNOT

To begin any crochet, you need to make a slip knot on the hook. The slip knot needs to be movable, so don't pull it too tight. Leave a tail long enough for weaving in; 6in (15cm) should suffice.

Step 1
Lay the tail end of the yarn over the ball end, creating a loop. Insert the hook through the loop, grab the working yarn with it, and pull it through to make a loop on the hook.

Step 2
Tighten the loop by tugging on the ball end and tail end at the same time. So that the slip knot fits snugly on the hook, pull on the tail end gently. Make sure you don't pull too tight; the loop on the hook needs to move freely.

HOLDING THE YARN

The left hand (if you are right-handed) controls the yarn. It is important to maintain an even tension on the yarn.

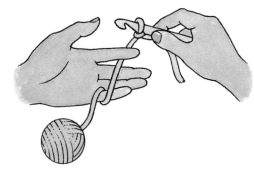

Step 1
Wind the yarn around your pinky finger and place the working yarn over your index finger. Alternatively, hold the tension by locking the yarn between your pinky and ring finger, and place the working yarn over the index finger.

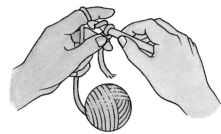

Step 2
To make a stitch, use the hand holding the hook to maneuver it to wrap the yarn over the hook. Then with thumb and middle finger of your left hand, hold onto the tail to keep the work still and open as you pull the yarn through the loop on the hook.

LEFT-HANDED

If you are left-handed, hold the hook in your left hand and the yarn in your right hand, mirroring the instructions above.

FOUNDATION CHAIN

Tunisian crochet always begins with a foundation chain. This is a row of crochet chains that the Tunisian stitches will be worked into. Chains that form part of a stitch pattern are worked in the same way.

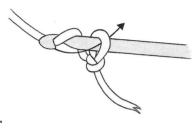

Step 1
Making sure that the tip of the hook faces downward (this helps the hook to slide through the loop easily), wrap the yarn over the hook in a counterclockwise direction. Pull the wrapped loop through the slip knot loop on the hook to make one chain.

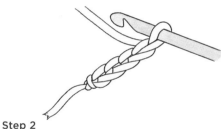

Step 2
Continue until you have made the desired number of chains.

UNDERSTANDING MULTIPLES

When making the foundation chain, it is important that you make the correct number of chain stitches for the pattern you are going to work. This number is given as a multiple before the instructions for each stitch. The multiple consists of the number of stitches required for each pattern repeat, plus any extra stitches needed to balance the pattern. For example, 'Multiple 4 sts + 3' means any number that divides by 4, with 3 more added, such as 8 + 3 (a total of 11) or 44 + 3 (a total of 47).

The front of the foundation chain looks like a series of Vs or little hearts, while the back of the chain forms a distinctive bump of yarn behind each V. Count each V-shaped loop on the front of the chain as one chain stitch, but do not count the slip knot or the loop that is on the hook. You can also turn the chain over and count the stitches on the back if you find that easier.

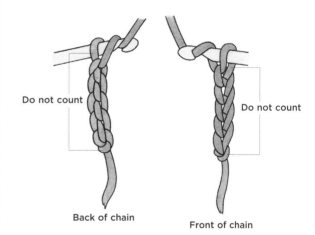

Do not count

Do not count

Back of chain

Front of chain

THE IMPORTANCE OF GAUGE

Gauge is the number of stitches (or pattern repeats) and rows (or rounds) to a given measurement, usually 1, 2, or 4in (2.5, 5, or 10cm). For your work to be the correct size, the gauge specified in the pattern must be matched as closely as possible.

Gauge not only depends on hook and yarn, but also on personal technique. Just because a pattern recommends a certain hook size does not necessarily mean that your gauge will be the same, which is why it is vital to always make a swatch and measure the gauge before you start your project, especially if it is a garment.

Measuring gauge
Work a piece of Tunisian crochet larger than 4 x 4in (10 x 10cm), usually around 6 x 6in (15 x 15cm). This will give you enough space to correctly count the stitches and rows.

Lay the swatch on a flat surface, using a tape measure and pins to mark out the desired size over which the gauge needs to be measured. Count exactly how many stitches and rows are within this square.

If you have more stitches or rows, this means you are a tight crocheter, so increase your hook size. If you have fewer stitches or rows, this means you are a loose crocheter, so go down a hook size.

FOUNDATION ROW

After making a foundation chain of the required length, you will work a foundation row consisting of a forward and return pass. All foundation rows are worked the same as Tunisian simple stitch unless instructed otherwise. You can work the forward pass into either the front or back of the chain; the back has been used in this book.

Forward pass
Starting in the second chain from the hook, roll the chain toward you and insert the hook into the back bump. Yarn over and pull through (2 loops on hook).

Return pass
Do not turn the work. Yarn over and pull through one loop on hook (this forms a locking chain). Then *yo and pull through 2 loops on hook.

Continue inserting the hook into each chain and pulling up a loop until you reach the end of the foundation chain.

Repeat from * until one loop is left on the hook. Use this method for all return passes on all rows unless the pattern specifies otherwise.

FORWARD AND RETURN PASSES

Each row of Tunisian crochet is made up of a forward pass and then a return pass. Note that you do not turn the work in Tunisian crochet; both forward and return passes are worked with the right side of the work facing you.

On the forward pass, worked from right to left, all the loops that are made are kept on the hook. These loops form the vertical bars of the stitch (see below). On the return pass, worked from left to right, the loops are worked off the hook in turn, leaving a single loop on the hook at the end of the pass. The return pass creates the chains that form the horizontal bars of the stitches.

FIRST AND LAST STITCHES

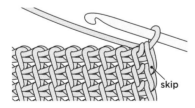

Skip first stitch
The loop left on the hook at the end of each return pass counts as the first stitch of the next forward pass, which means you should skip the first vertical bar on each subsequent forward pass. The patterns indicate this with the instruction "skip first vertical bar."

Work end stitch
The end stitch on the forward pass is always worked by inserting the hook under the front vertical bar at the edge of the fabric and the back vertical bar that lies directly behind it (2 bars on hook). Work a Tunisian simple stitch in the end stitch (yarn over and pull through) unless the pattern instructs otherwise.

ANATOMY OF A TUNISIAN STITCH

The key to Tunisian stitches lies in where you insert the hook, so it is important to be able to identify the different bars of the stitch.

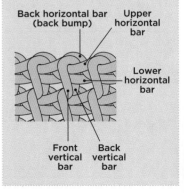

Back horizontal bar (back bump) — Upper horizontal bar — Lower horizontal bar — Front vertical bar — Back vertical bar

BASIC STITCHES AND VARIATIONS

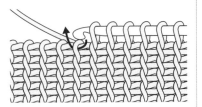

Tunisian simple stitch
Insert hook from right to left under front vertical bar of stitch, yo and pull through.

Return pass (for all basic sts)
Yo and pull through 1 loop on hook, *yo and pull through 2 loops; rep from * until 1 loop left on hook.

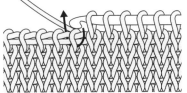

Tunisian knit stitch
Insert hook from front to back through center of stitch between front and back vertical bars, yo and pull through.

To work a different stitch "as for Tks," insert the hook as above.

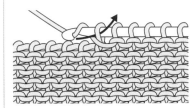

Tunisian purl stitch
Bring yarn to front, insert hook from right to left under front vertical bar of stitch, take yarn across front of stitch to back of work, yo and pull through.

To work a different stitch "as for Tps," move the yarn and insert the hook as above.

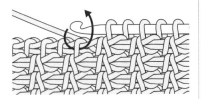

Twisted simple stitch
Using tip of hook, grasp next vertical bar, twist hook up to right, yo and pull through. This example shows twisted simple stitches alternated with regular simple stitches.

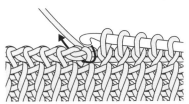

Twisted knit stitch
Using tip of hook, pull front vertical bar to right until you see back vertical bar, insert hook from front to back through center of stitch between vertical bars, yo and pull through.

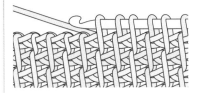

Tunisian slip stitch
Insert hook from right to left under front vertical bar of stitch and leave bar on hook without working it. This example shows slip stitches alternated with simple stitches.

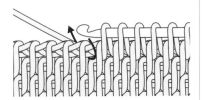

Tunisian full stitch
Insert hook from front to back in space between stitches (or in chain space or other indicated space), yo and pull through.

To work a different stitch "as for Tfs," insert the hook as above.

Tunisian reverse stitch
With yarn and hook at back, insert hook from right to left under back vertical bar of stitch, yo and pull through.

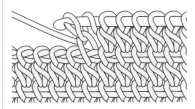

Tunisian double crochet
Yo and insert hook as for simple stitch (unless specified otherwise). Yo and pull through, yo and pull through 2 loops on hook only. Ch 1 at beginning of row to give the correct height for the stitch and work a double into the end stitch. Other standard crochet stitches can be worked using the same principle.

Special Stitches and Techniques

DECREASES

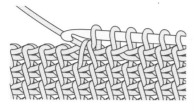

Work stitches together (Tss2tog)
The best method is to work two (or more) stitches together. In Tunisian simple stitch: insert hook under 2 (or more) vertical bars at same time, yo and pull through.

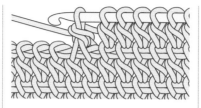

Work stitches together (Tdc2tog)
To work two (or more) Tunisian doubles together: yo, insert hook under 2 front vertical bars at same time, yo and pull through, yo and pull through 2 loops.

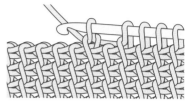

Skip a stitch
This is a simple way to decrease, but note that it creates a visible space.

INCREASES

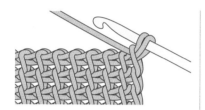

At right edge
Work one stitch into the first vertical bar (the one that is usually skipped).

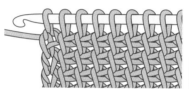

At left edge
Make one extra stitch by inserting the hook under the last upper and back horizontal bars before the end stitch, yo and pull through.

Anywhere in a row
This increase is worked as for Tunisian full stitch: insert hook in space between stitches, yo and pull through.

LACEWORK AND YARN OVERS

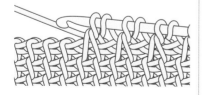

Step 1
Wrap the yarn over the hook and work the next stitch. The yarn over creates an eyelet and counts as a stitch. Here, it is followed by a decrease (Tss2tog) to keep the stitch count correct.

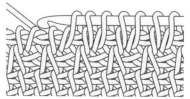

Step 2
On the next forward pass, fill the yarn over space by inserting the hook into the space and work as for Tunisian full stitch.

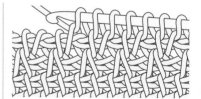

Step 3
Alternatively, insert the hook under the front leg of the yarn over and work as for Tunisian simple stitch.

CLUSTERS

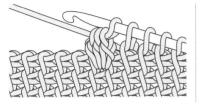

Bobble

This is a type of cluster formed by working several Tunisian double crochet (or longer) stitches together in one stitch. Make sure you pop the finished cluster to the front of the work. To make a 3 Tdc bobble: [yo, insert hook as instructed, yo and pull through, yo and pull through 2 loops] 3 times, yo and pull through all 3 loops on hook.

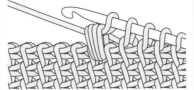

Puff

A puff is normally a group of three or more half double crochets worked in one stitch, which are then joined together at the top. To make a puff: *yo, insert hook as instructed, yo and pull through; rep from * as many times as required, then yo and pull through all created loops. Often ch 1 is worked to lock the puff.

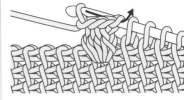

Popcorn

A popcorn is a group of doubles worked in one stitch, then the top of the first stitch is joined to the last to make the popcorn. To make a 4 Tdc popcorn: [yo, insert hook as instructed, yo and pull through, yo and pull through 2 loops, [yo, insert hook in same st, yo and pull through, (yo and pull through 2 loops) twice] 3 times. Slip last loop off hook, insert hook in top of first stitch made, catch empty loop and pull through, ch 1 to lock the popcorn.

FANS AND SHELLS

These decorative stitches are made in the same way as increases and decreases, but they are offset with added chains or skipped stitches to always keep the correct number of stitches.

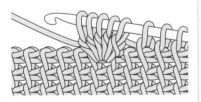

Fans

These are created on forward passes, and are usually Tunisian double crochet (or longer) stitches. To make a 5 Tdc fan: skip 2 sts, [yo, insert hook as instructed, yo and pull through, yo and pull through 2 loops] 5 times, skip next 2 sts.

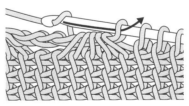

Shells

Shells are mostly created on return passes. Make enough chains before and after the shell to keep the correct number of stitches. To make a 5 stitch shell on the return pass: *ch 2, yo and pull through 6 loops, ch 2. Note that the working loop (the loop at the end of the hook) counts as 1, plus the 5 stitches that will form the shell. On the next forward pass, work into the horizontal loop at the top of the shell.

CABLES

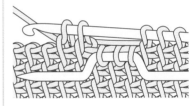

Cables are created by slipping a number of stitches onto a cable needle and placing them at the front or back of the work; work the next stitches on the main fabric, then work the stitches from the cable needle, creating twists.

Cables might look complicated, but once you get started you will realize it is a simple technique to master. In this book most of the cables are worked in Tunisian simple stitch on a background of Tunisian purl stitch, which makes the cables more prominent.

JOINING YARN AND CHANGING COLORS

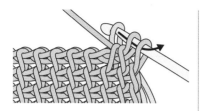

At end of return pass
When you have two loops left on the hook, wrap the new yarn over the hook and finish off the return pass with the new yarn.

At end of forward pass
Finish off the forward pass with the old yarn and then work the first "yo and pull through" of the return pass with the new yarn.

CARRYING YARNS

When working in short stripes, do not cut the yarn at the end of every stripe. Instead, carry it up the side of the work and use it when necessary. This is faster and leaves fewer ends to weave in. The yarn you are carrying has to be on the same side on every change.

BINDING OFF

This gives the work a neat edge, although it is not always necessary. Some shawl patterns end the project after the final return pass to give a stretchier edge. To bind off, you will work a standard crochet slip stitch. This example is shown on Tunisian simple stitch, but you should cast off by inserting the hook as per the stitch type.

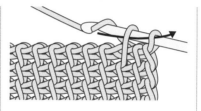

Step 1
Skip first vertical bar, then insert hook in next vertical bar, yo and pull through stitch and loop on hook.

Step 2
Repeat until all stitches have been worked. You will finish with one loop on the hook, ready to fasten off.

FASTENING OFF AND WEAVING IN

To fasten off the yarn securely, work one chain, then cut the yarn leaving a tail approximately 6in (15cm) long for weaving in. Pull the tail through the loop and tighten. Weave in tails on the wrong side of the work.

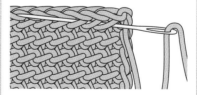

Step 1
Thread the tail through a tapestry needle and take the needle through several stitches (three should suffice).

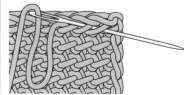

Step 2
Then work back on yourself, omitting the last stitch and making sure the yarn is trapped between stitches.

BLOCKING

The term blocking describes a process of wetting, laying, and drying the project. It is a vital step in Tunisian crochet to open up the pattern and showcase it to its full potential. It also helps the pieces to keep their shape.

Steam blocking

Pin the piece to the desired size on a towel or ironing board and steam it with an iron, being very careful not to touch the fabric. Hover the iron slowly over the item, making sure the steam penetrates the fibers. Allow to dry naturally. Be careful when steam blocking acrylic items, as too much heat from the iron can permanently damage the fibers in the yarn. Steam block cables with the wrong side facing upward or you will flatten the cables.

Wet blocking

This method is perfect for shawls, as it opens up the lace sections beautifully. Soak the item in lukewarm water with a drop of wool wash, squeeze out the water (do not wring the item), and place the project on a dry towel. Roll it in the towel and pat the excess moisture out. Pin the item on a towel or blocking mat to the size required. Allow to dry naturally.

Spray blocking

This is the mildest form of wet blocking and works for all fibers. Right side up, pin the crochet to shape on a padded surface. Fill a spray bottle with cool tap water and spritz a fine, even mist over the piece. Use your hands to gently pat the moisture into the project. Allow to dry naturally.

DEALING WITH THE CURL

Tunisian crochet is significantly thicker than standard crochet or knitting. In lots of stitches the thickness lies at the back of the work, resulting in the fabric being heavier at the back and curling at the front. Tunisian stitches such as knit stitch will curl more than others; purl stitch on the other hand produces a fabric with no curl at all.

Blocking helps a lot with taming the curl, but also try using a bigger hook, which will make the stitches looser.

You can always crochet a small border to stop the edges from curling as well; also try to keep the foundation chains fairly loose.

SEAMS

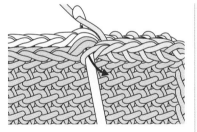

Slip stitch

Holding the pieces to be joined with right sides together, insert the hook into the stitches of both pieces. Yo and pull through both stitches, ch 1; this locks the pieces together. Insert hook under edge stitches of both pieces, yo and pull through stitches and loop on hook. You can work the seam in single crochet in the same way.

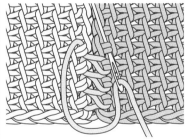

Mattress stitch—method 1

Place pieces side by side, right sides uppermost, and thread the yarn through a tapestry needle. Insert needle through corner of one piece, then through corner of the other. Insert needle under horizontal bars of stitch closest to the edge. Mirror this on the other piece. Continue in pairs, working each stitch on each side.

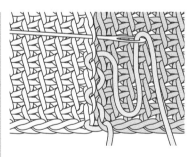

Mattress stitch—method 2

This is the same as method 1, but this time work into the edge stitches. On one piece, insert needle from front to back into first stitch and then from back to front into center of next stitch. Mirror this on the other piece. Continue in pairs, working each stitch on each side.

TUNISIAN CROCHET SKILLS

Symbols and Abbreviations

These are the abbreviations and symbols used in this book. There is no worldwide standard, so you may find different abbreviations and symbols in other publications. Always read the list provided with the pattern you are using before starting a project. Note that American crochet terms are used throughout this book.

ABBREVIATIONS

Below is an alphabetical list of abbreviations used in the written patterns in this book.

Abbreviation	Meaning
C4B or C6B, C4F or C6F	cable 4 or 6 back, cable 4 or 6 front; these use a cable needle (like knitting) and are explained with the relevant patterns (the same applies to twists below)
ch	chain
CL	cluster
ETks	extended Tunisian knit stitch
ETss	extended Tunisian simple stitch
rep	repeat
sl st	slip stitch
sp(s)	space(s)
st(s)	stitch(es)
T3B or T4B	twist 3 or 4 back
T3F or T4F	twist 3 or 4 front
Tdc	Tunisian double crochet
Tfpdc	Tunisian front post double crochet
Tfs	Tunisian full stitch
Tks	Tunisian knit stitch
tog	together
Tps	Tunisian purl stitch
Trs	Tunisian reverse stitch
Tslst	Tunisian slip stitch
Tss	Tunisian simple stitch
Ttr	Tunisian treble crochet
TwTks	twisted Tunisian knit stitch
TwTss	twisted Tunisian simple stitch
yo	yarn over
yu	yarn under
[ ]	repeat instructions within brackets number of times stated

BASIC STITCHES

See pages 164–165 for instructions on how to work the basic stitches.

Stitch	Abbreviation	Symbol
chain	ch	◯
return pass	-	∼
Tunisian simple stitch	Tss	│
Tss worked into end stitch	work end st	‖
Tunisian knit stitch	Tks	◯
Tunisian purl stitch	Tps	─
Tunisian full stitch	Tfs	⏀
Tunisian reverse stitch	Trs	⏚
Tunisian slip stitch	Tslst	∨
Tunisian double crochet	Tdc	ⵜ

BASIC STITCH VARIATIONS

Many stitch patterns use special stitch constructions and, where these occur in this book, the abbreviation is indicated in the special stitch instructions near the beginning of the pattern. Always refer to special stitch instructions where they occur. Any published pattern should include a list of all the abbreviations and symbols used, which may differ from those used in this book.

Description	Abbreviation	Symbol	Description	Abbreviation	Symbol
extended Tunisian simple stitch	ETss (work 1 Tss, ch 1)		Tunisian simple stitch plus chains	e.g. 1 Tss, ch 4	
extended Tunisian knit stitch	ETks (work 1 Tks, ch 1)		stitch worked around post (both vertical bars) from front of work	e.g. Tfpdc (Tunisian front post double crochet)	
Tunisian knit stitch purled	Tks purled (work with yarn in front as for Tps)		Tunisian treble crochet	Ttr	
Tunisian slip stitch purled	Tslst purled (work with yarn in front as for Tps)		stitch worked into a row below	e.g. long Tdc or long Ttr	or
twisted Tunisian simple stitch	TwTss				
twisted Tunisian knit stitch	TwTks		standard crochet slip stitch	sl st	
insert hook as for Tfs	e.g. 1 ETss or 1 Tdc worked as for Tfs	or	picot	e.g. ch 3, sl st in next st	
insert hook in chain	e.g. 1 Tss in ch		yarn over	yo	
insert hook in horizontal bar	e.g. 1 Tss in horizontal bar		double yarn over	[yo] twice	
insert hook in loop at top of stitch, shell, or cluster	e.g. 1 Tss in top of shell		yarn under	yu	

INCREASES, DECREASES, WRAPPED, AND CROSSED STITCHES

Increases and decreases are used to create decorative stitches and for shaping. Combined with yarn overs, they form the basis of many lace, wave, and chevron patterns. Yarn overs also create the central space in V stitches, and can be used to wrap other stitches for texture and pattern. Crossed stitches (working stitches out of order rather than consecutively) also create decorative relief effects.

Description	Abbreviation	Symbol	Description	Abbreviation	Symbol
simple stitch increase	e.g. 2 Tss in next st		simple stitch decrease	e.g. Tss2tog	or
double crochet increase, e.g. to create a fan	e.g. 5 Tdc in next st		purled simple stitch decrease	e.g. Tss2tog purled (work with yarn in front as for Tps)	
double crochet increase, e.g. to create a half fan	e.g. 3 Tdc in next st		simple stitch decrease on return pass	yo and pull through working loop plus 2 sts	
simple V stitch	simple V st: e.g. [1 Tss, yo, 1 Tss] in next st		simple stitch decrease	Tss3tog	
simple V stitch in loop at top of stitch, shell, or cluster	e.g. simple V st in top of shell		simple stitch decrease on return pass to make a shell	yo and pull through working loop plus 3 sts	
double V stitch	double V st: e.g. [1 Tdc, yo, 1 Tdc] in next st		double crochet decrease	e.g. Tdc2tog	
increase in loop at top of stitch, shell, or cluster	e.g. [1 Tss, yo, 1 Tss, yo, 1 Tss] in top of shell		decrease with substitute stitch	e.g. Tdc2tog, 1 Tdc in next sp	
one wrapped simple stitch	yo, 1 Tss, lift yo over Tss		crossed Tunisian simple stitch	crossed Tss	
two wrapped simple stitches	yo, 2 Tss, lift yo over 2 Tss		crossed Tunisian knit stitch	crossed Tks	
three wrapped simple stitches	yo, 3 Tss, lift yo over 3 Tss		crossed Tunisian double stitch	crossed Tdc	

CLUSTERS AND CABLES

Clusters are decorative stitches gathered at the top or at both top and bottom, and are used to make interesting effects such as bobbles, puffs, and popcorns. Star stitches are made by gathering a group of stitches (a decrease) and then immediately increasing in the same stitches to form a star. Cables are a beautiful way of adding texture and interest to any pattern.

Description	Abbreviation	Symbol	Description	Abbreviation	Symbol
cluster	CL: e.g. Tdc3tog in next st		star stitch of specified number of stitches	e.g. Tss5tog star	
bobble	e.g. Tdc5tog in next st		three stitch cable	T3st cable	
popcorn	e.g. work 5 doubles in next st, close at top, ch 1		cable 4 front	C4F	
puff	e.g. hdc4tog in next st		cable 4 back	C4B	
puff worked by inserting hook as for Tfs	e.g. hdc3tog in next st (as for Tfs)		cable 6 front	C6F	
open puff with specified number of loops	OP: e.g. of 3 or 6 loops		cable 6 back	C6B	
closing an open puff on return pass	e.g. yo and pull through loop on hook plus 3 or 6 sts		twist 3 front	T3F	
cluster worked into specifed row below	long CL: e.g. Tdc2tog in next st 3 rows below)		twist 3 back	T3B	
claw: stitches worked into rows below and joined at top	e.g. Ttr3tog in specified rows below		twist 4 front	T4F	
			twist 4 back	T4B	

Index

INDEX

174

Credits

All photographs and illustrations are the copyright of Quarto Publishing plc. While every effort has been made to credit contributors, Quarto would like to apologize should there have been any omissions or errors—and would be pleased to make the appropriate correction for future editions of the book.

SUPPLIER
We would like to thank Rowan for generously supplying the yarn used to make the swatches in this book.

knitrowan.com

Rowan Summerlite DK, 100% cotton
• Basic stitches: 479 Giggle, 463 Pear
• Fans and shells: 476 Duckling,
    453 Summer, 475 Pickles
• Bobbles and clusters: 460 Linen,
    456 Cantaloupe, 473 Nutkin
• Cables: 462 Rouge, 474 Piglet
• Relief stitches: 451 Mocha, 452 Plaster,
    467 Coral Blush, 458 Steel, 454 Mushroom
• Lace stitches: 455 Fuchsia, 472 Pink Powder,
    468 Silvery Blue, 478 Moon
• Waves and chevrons: 469 Favourite Denim,
    457 Lagoon, 459 Ocean
• Embellishments: 466 Seashell

AUTHOR'S ACKNOWLEDGMENTS
Huge thank you to the wonderful Quarto team, Kate, Michelle, Martina, and everyone who worked on this book. Phil for his amazing photography. Rowan for providing the yarns and anyone who had a contribution in making this book so fantastic.

Also, big thank you to my wonderful husband, Dave, for his constant love and support. To my sister, Kate, for her honesty and encouragement.